Dancing
on the Table

*Easily Elegant Recipes
to Keep the Joy in Entertaining*

THE JUNIOR LEAGUE OF WILMINGTON

𝒯he Junior League of Wilmington, Inc. is an organization of women committed to promoting voluntarism, developing the potential of women, and improving communities through the effective action and leadership of trained volunteers. Its purpose is exclusively educational and charitable.

~ *JLW Mission Statement*

To order copies of

Dancing on the Table

please contact JLW Headquarters:
1801 North Market Street
Wilmington, DE 19802

office: (302) 652-3700
fax: (302) 652-0826

E-Mail: JuniorLeague@diamondnet.org

ISBN: 0-9714833-0-2

WIMMER
C O O K B O O K S
ConsolidatedGraphics

1-800-548-2537

Table of Contents

Introduction

Never doubt that a small group of thoughtful, committed citizens
can change the world. Indeed, it is the only thing that ever has.

~ Margaret Mead

... And that's where this cookbook began. With an idea that waltzed through the minds of an enthusiastic group of volunteers, who realize that given the resources, they can produce as much magic as the pairing of Ginger Rogers and Fred Astaire. *Dancing on the Table* was choreographed to be an indispensable partner in the kitchen, and a valuable partner in the Junior League of Wilmington's projects throughout the community.

Dancing on the Table is a very special collection of our favorite recipes, all triple-tested, and orchestrated to be a pleasure to cook from and a delight to share. It features easily elegant recipes that are perfect for family or entertaining, topped off with presentation ideas, cooking tips, time-saving strategies, and other information every host and hostess can use. But like any appealing dance, it's so much more than just the steps. It's also the First Official Cookbook of the State of Delaware, spiced throughout with lovely photographs and interesting information about the region. From the "Chateau Country" of the beautiful Brandywine Valley, to the Delaware beaches and Bay, we're pleased to bring you the full flavor of The First State.

The Junior League of Wilmington extends its warmest thanks to Governor Ruth Ann Minner and Senator Thomas R. Carper, as well as to the Delaware Economic Development Office, the Delaware Tourism Office, and the many fine museums in our area. Without them, we wouldn't have been able to serve up this buffet of fascinating tidbits about the state and its attractions. In addition, the Cookbook Committee would like to thank the Board and members of the Junior League of Wilmington, whose fabulous recipes and thoughtful support have guided this project from the beginning. We also appreciate their testing each and every recipe along the way!

And finally, we would like to thank you. By purchasing this cookbook, you too, are a partner in the dance. Proceeds from the sale of this book will support the many worthwhile community projects sponsored by the Junior League of Wilmington. We appreciate your support, and hope that you will invite your family and friends to join the party by ordering additional copies of *Dancing on the Table*.

About the Illustrator

The creative talent behind our illustrations is Libby Wendorf. Libby was an Active member of the Junior League of Wilmington for five years, participating in our American Girls Fashion Show, the Whale of a Sale, and as co-chair for the Provisional Class. She has recently moved to Wisconsin with her husband and daughter, and is currently volunteering with the Junior League of Milwaukee. Nonetheless, Libby didn't hesitate to give generously of her time and talents, providing us with original artwork for the cover and illustrations throughout the book. Her whimsical drawings have captured the essence of *Dancing on the Table*, and we are most appreciative!

Although Libby has taken an occasional art class, the majority of her formal training was in music and elementary education. However, she has always enjoyed visiting museums, and her artistic skills are largely self-taught. Her character drawings began as doodles in junior high school. In college, she began creating her own Christmas cards for family and friends, a tradition that continues today. *Dancing on the Table* is her first published work.

The Junior League of Wilmington

White gloves and pearls. Tea parties. Former debutantes doing good deeds. These traditional images of the Junior League persist in movies and on TV. The reality, however, is quite different. Today's Junior League member could be a single professional, a working mother, a student, or a stay-at-home mom. In fact, many Junior League members play more than one of these roles during their League careers. And as members of the League, they are able to serve as volunteers, mentors, and leaders as well. The League provides a wide variety of opportunities for education, service, creativity, and friendship for women, as they pass through the phases of their lives. League members come from varied backgrounds to pool their talents and experience, in order to effect positive change in their communities.

The Junior League of Wilmington, founded in 1918, has provided nearly a century's worth of community service, with over 700 Active and Sustaining members contributing 20,000 volunteer hours per year to the greater Wilmington area. Our focus has been to promote women's issues, child advocacy, opportunities and services for older adults, the alleviation of homelessness, and an ever-improving quality of life in our community. Traditionally, the League has begun or boosted fledgling organizations, and withdrawn when these organizations were able to function on their own. Throughout the years, the League has renewed its affiliation with many organizations, and participated in numerous coalitions. The following are the most significant projects of the Junior League of Wilmington:

1920s:
Well Baby Clinic and Health Center
Delaware School for Deaf Children
Wilmington Waterways
Italian Settlement (now West End Neighborhood House)
Children's Bureau
Theater Puppet Committee
Children's Play Committee
Girls' Industrial School

1930s:
Mayor's Committee for Relief during the Depression
Summer Food Relief
Children's Bureau
Delaware School for Deaf Children
West End Neighborhood House
Wilmington Society for the Fine Arts
Delaware Art Center

1940s:
West End Neighborhood House
Children's Home
Delaware School for Deaf Children
U.S.O.

Women's Division War Finance Committee
Christmas Stocking
Delaware Curative Workshop

1950s:
Child Guidance Center
Christmas Clearing House
Delaware Curative Workshop
Theater Puppet Committee
Radio & TV Committee produced series of
  children's programs
Wilmington Senior Center
Delaware Art Museum docent service

1960s:
Delaware Art Museum Children's Gallery
Fun Books
Historic Preservation Survey for Historical Society
  of Delaware
Delaware Nature Education Society and Ashland
  Nature Center
Child Diagnostic and Development Center of
  Delaware and Jefferson Pre-School
SERVE (Seniors Engaged in Regular Volunteer
  Efforts) at the Wilmington Senior Center

DAPI (Delaware Adolescent Program, Inc.)
Theater Puppet Committee, Wilmington Senior Center

1970s:
PEG (Preventive Environmental for Girls, Inc.)
POST (Parents Organized for Support and Training)
Historic Preservation brochure with Delaware
  Ethnic Studies and Culture, Inc.
Art to the Hospitals
DAPI advocacy committee
"Right to Read" School Volunteer tutor program,
  Wilmington Square
Wilmington Senior Center
CIP (Concern for Children in Placement)
Brandywine House (elderly congregate living facility)
"Permanency, Security and Love" (children's rights
  conference)
"For Our Children" brochure
"Mini Museums" from Metropolitan Museum of Art
CAN (Child Advocacy Newsletter)
Grand Opera House Victorian staircase (JLW 60th
  Anniversary)
Lecture: "A Family Foundation: Today's Child,
  Tomorrow's Adult"

1980s:
Rockwood Museum
"Sharing, Caring, Loving: Your Baby and You"
  Parenting manual, Parents Anonymous of
  Delaware, Inc.
Ashland Nature Center Discovery Room
Guardian Ad Litem Program
Public School Volunteers
Hospice newsletter, library and Speaker's Bureau
POST (Parents Organized for Support and Training)
Women's History Week
Child, Inc.
Waterfront Task Force, Wilmington Waterways
  (Waterfest Children's Corner)
Delaware Women's Conference
Alfred I. DuPont Auxiliary (& Red Balloon Gift Shop)
Poplar Street Greenspace
Bubbylonian Encounter
Delaware Children's Theatre
The Prevention Project
"Woman to Woman"
Wilmington Institute Public Library

Senior Citizens Health Care Booklet with the
  Wilmington Senior Center
"Foster Care Review Act" series
"We Care in Delaware" with the Ronald McDonald
  House
Women's Legislative Roundtable sponsor
Hallmark's Kaleidoscope creative art workshop
Franny Maguire, JLW member, testified about foster
  care before two U.S. Congressional subcommittees
Parents as Teachers pilot with Parent Early
  Education Center
Distribution of ChildSafe Tape by Video Matrix
Reportline
Selected Teen Outreach
Ronald McDonald House (fundraising raffle at
  LPGA McDonald's Championship)
Ad-Hoc Task Force on Homelessness
Read-Aloud Delaware
Delaware Children's Museum

1990's
YWCA Project Self-Sufficiency
Adolescent Parent Advocates
ARC Adolescent Clinic
Child, Inc.
Community Legal Aid Society, Inc.
Supporting K.I.D.D.S.
West End Neighborhood House
Immunization Public Awareness Campaign
"Bridges for Play" JLW 75th Anniversary
  Playground Project
Multicultural Task Force
Delaware Women's Conference
Delaware Children's Museum
Read-Aloud Delaware
Ronald McDonald House (fundraising raffle at
  LPGA McDonald's Championship)
Wellness Community Delaware
ARC House (Association for the Rights of Citizens
  with Mental Retardation)
YWCA Mural
Restoration of the Monkey Hill Pavilion

2000s:
Association for Rights of Citizens
CHILD, Inc.
Delaware Adolescent Program, Inc.
Ronald McDonald House, Inc.

Junior League of Wilmington Headquarters

The Junior League of Wilmington is headquartered in the Lea-Derickson House, at 1801 North Market Street in Wilmington, Delaware. We are proud to play a part in the life of this historic property.

In the early 1770s, miller John Marshall built the Lea-Derickson house using stone taken from the bed of the north race of the Brandywine River. The simple facade is typical of the Quaker-Georgian architecture of the surrounding Brandywine Village area. James Marshall had financial difficulties and sold the house to Samuel Morton, another merchant miller, who in turn sold it to Thomas Lea around 1785. In the mid-1830s a well-to-do miller, Jacob Derickson, bought the house as a wedding gift for his daughter, Martha. The property remained in the Derickson family until its sale to Old Brandywine Village, Inc., in 1963. During those 130 years there were several additions to the house, which doubled its original size.

In 1962, this house and others on the 1800 block of Market Street were to be razed to allow for construction of a motel. A group of citizens, including Mrs. Charles Reese, a Junior League past-president, formed Old Brandywine Village, Inc. (OBV), a non-profit organization whose purpose was to restore the historic homes in this area and to insure their future. 1801 Market Street was purchased by OBV in 1963 and restored under the direction of architect Robert Raley. Some of the artifacts that were discovered on the property by the Archaeological Society of Delaware are displayed in the living room of the house.

The Junior League of Wilmington leased the Lea-Derickson house from Old Brandywine Village, Inc., in 1965, and established its headquarters in this historic building. On August 6, 1981, the Junior League assumed ownership of the house. The house is an excellent example of a private home of historic value that has been preserved and renovated for a use other than originally intended, while retaining important architectural features.

The Cookbook Committee wishes to extend its thanks to the members and Board of the Junior League of Wilmington, for their support, guidance, enthusiasm, and many hours of testing and tasting recipes.

Cookbook Committee
2000 ~ 2001

Co-Chairs
Betts Murdison and Kate Zabriskie

Recipe Chair
Renée Bosco

Text & Design Chair
Patsy Keller

Committee Members
Keia Benefield

Shelley Boden

Jeanine Cillo

Kate Davis

Terri Greenley

Karen Hammond

Heather Hayter

Tammy Holm

Laurie Johnson

Suzy Johnson

Dinah Kirby

Laura Macauley

Gina Mancini-Becker

Kimberly Martin

Lyn Milliman

Shannon Oates

Lisa Quadrini

Dawn Ryan

Jean Smith

Jamie Stanzione

Deb Thoet

Cover Photo

The cover photo for *Dancing on the Table* was taken at the home of Jan Norman, near Hockessin, Delaware. This "bank barn," built into the side of a hill with ground level entrances on each floor, dates from the Civil War era. The Normans began renovating the barn in 1976, and today it is a beautiful 6,500 square foot home, overlooking the lake at Bridleshire Farms.

The grand piano sits at one end of the 19x35-foot living room, which was originally a hayloft. It overlooks a spiral staircase to the dining room below, which is graced with fieldstone walls and a 24-foot ceiling. The barn's original structure and materials were used whenever possible, from stone pillars and walls to the hand-hewn beams, giving the home a spacious, yet rustic, elegance.

The Junior League of Wilmington would like to thank Jan for providing this lovely setting for our cover photo.

We also appreciate the generosity of the two local businesses ~ Everything But The Kitchen Sink, and Simon Pearce on the Brandywine ~ that allowed us to use the beautiful china, crystal, silver, and hand-blown glass that dance across our tabletop.

Everything But The Kitchen Sink is located in Hockessin. The site was originally a hardware store, with stone-walled bins for grain and coal storage. In 1977, the store opened as a small gift shop in two sections of the six-bay coal bins. Today, it spills out into the second floor loft, where railcars were once winched up to deposit coal below. As the name implies, Everything But The Kitchen Sink offers a wide variety of traditional to contemporary pieces, including anything a host or hostess would need to set a beautiful table.

The original, hand-blown glass shown in the photo is from Simon Pearce on the Brandywine. Located in West Chester, Pennsylvania, Simon Pearce combines a glassblowing workshop with a restaurant and retail store. Visitors can watch as artisans create clear glass pieces of exquisite quality. Every piece is an original Simon Pearce design, created with two things in mind: beauty and function. Shown are the Hartland Star Bowl, the Pomfret Pitcher, and a small Star Bowl.

The cover photograph was taken by Heather Hayter and Patsy Keller.

Tap Dancing ~ Appetizers

Above: Flower Garden Walk
at Longwood Gardens

Right: Main Fountains at Longwood

Tap Dancing
Appetizers

Flower Garden Walk at Longwood Gardens

What better place for tea than among the tulips? Longwood Gardens encompasses 1,050 acres of beautiful gardens, woodlands and meadows. In April, the 600-foot long Flower Garden Walk, shown here, is a rainbow ranging from deep purples and pinks, to red, orange, yellow and white in a progression of color for the spring season. Throughout the gardens, 6,500 varieties of plants are grown, and in early spring, more than two million minor bulbs bloom near the Oak Knoll, creating a soft blanket of color.

*Photograph by Heather Hayter
and Patsy Keller*

Main Fountains at Longwood

Three major fountain gardens combine European elegance and American ingenuity. The Open Air Theatre, the Italian Water Garden, and the Main Fountain Garden, shown here, utilize 1700 jets, sending water as high as 130 feet, and recirculating nearly 17,000 gallons of water per minute. Throughout the summer, there are daily fountain displays on the hour, with illuminated displays three nights a week. Several times each summer, visitors are thrilled by a spectacular display of fireworks and fountains, set to music.

*Photograph courtesy of
Longwood Gardens: L. Albee*

Smoky White Bean Dip

Serves 10 to 12

1 (16 ounce) can cannellini (white beans), drained
1 tablespoon chipotle pepper sauce
2 tablespoons freshly squeezed lime juice
2 teaspoons liquid smoke
1 clove garlic, pressed
2 tablespoons fresh cilantro leaves
Salt to taste

Combine all the ingredients in a food processor until smooth. Serve with toasted pita bread.

Tapenade

Serves 10 to 12

1 pound pitted kalamata olives
½ cup capers
3 to 4 anchovies
2 pinches tuna fish
½ cup olive oil
1 tablespoon freshly squeezed lemon juice
1 small clove garlic

Layer the olives, capers, anchovies, tuna, olive oil, lemon juice, and garlic in a food processor. Pulse until the desired consistency. Serve with toast rounds.

Black Bean and Mango Salsa

Makes 4 cups

1 (15.5 ounce) can black beans, rinsed and drained
10 ounces frozen corn, thawed
1 cup diced mango, juice reserved
⅓ cup chopped fresh cilantro leaves
⅓ cup chopped red onion
¼ cup freshly squeezed lime juice
½ cup chopped red bell pepper
1 envelope dry good seasons dressing

Combine all the ingredients in a medium bowl. Cover and refrigerate until ready to use. Serve with chips or grilled chicken.

As the first state to ratify the United States Constitution, Delaware is always the first state to march in inaugural parades.

Life isn't a matter of milestones but of moments.
~ Rose Fitzgerald Kennedy

Black Bean Hummus
Serves 10 to 12

2 (15 ounce) cans black beans, rinsed and drained
¾ cup tahini
¼ cup freshly squeezed lemon juice
¼ cup packed, chopped fresh cilantro leaves
4 green onions, sliced
2 tablespoons olive oil
2 large cloves garlic, minced
1 teaspoon ground cumin
¾ teaspoon cayenne pepper
Salt to taste

Combine all the ingredients in a food processor until well blended. Transfer to a serving bowl, and serve with toasted pita triangles or fresh vegetables.

♪ *A nice variation on standard hummus.*

Smoked Trout Mousse
Serves 10 to 12

1 cup ricotta cheese, puréed until smooth
1 cup coarsely flaked smoked trout
2 tablespoons drained, prepared horseradish
2 tablespoons chopped fresh chives
1 tablespoon chopped fresh dill leaves
2 teaspoons freshly squeezed lemon juice
Salt and freshly ground black pepper to taste

Place the puréed ricotta in a medium bowl and carefully fold in half of the trout. Stir in the horseradish, chives, dill, and lemon juice, and then season with salt and pepper to taste. Fold in the remaining trout, incorporating thoroughly. Transfer the trout mixture to small crocks or jars, and chill until ready to use. Serve with Melba rounds, crackers, or croustades.

Toffee Dip with Apples

Serves 10 to 12

¾ cup packed dark brown sugar

½ cup confectioners' sugar

1 teaspoon pure vanilla extract

1 (8 ounce) block cream cheese, softened

¾ cup toffee bits

1 cup orange juice

6 Red Delicious apples, cored and cut into wedges

6 Granny Smith or Yellow Delicious apples, cored and cut into wedges

Combine the brown sugar, confectioners' sugar, vanilla, and cream cheese with an electric mixer, beating until smooth. Add the toffee bits and mix well. Place in a serving bowl, cover, and chill. Combine the orange juice and apple wedges in a bowl, and toss well to prevent the wedges from browning. Drain the apple wedges and arrange around the bowl of dip to serve.

♪ *As odd as this recipe may sound, this is so delicious.*
The original recipe used ⅓ less fat cream cheese
and also tasted great.

To keep a cutting board from moving while you chop fruit or vegetables, set it on a piece of non-slip mesh. Two types are readily available: The "non-slip" shelf liner found at grocery stores, and the rubber padding that's used to keep area rugs in place.

Hoagie Dip

Serves a crowd

¼ pound of ham, diced

¼ pound of capocollo, diced

¼ pound of provolone cheese, diced

¼ pound of American cheese, diced

2 medium tomatoes, chopped

1 small green bell pepper, chopped

1 small onion, chopped

1 tablespoon dried oregano

¼ cup oil

3 tablespoons mayonnaise

Combine the ham, capocollo, provolone, American cheese, tomatoes, green pepper, and onion in a medium mixing bowl. Sprinkle in the oregano and stir to incorporate. Stir in the oil, and then stir in the mayonnaise. Serve with French bread or crackers.

Delaware is truly a small wonder. It is only 96 miles long, and varies from 9 to 35 miles wide.

~

A piece of dental floss or fishing line, stretched taut, can split a cake into layers without a turntable and with a minimum of crumbs. It also slices a log of soft cheese into rounds that retain their shape.

Chicken Chutney Spread

Serves 6 to 8

1 cup chopped cooked chicken
½ cup mayonnaise, or more if desired
3 ounces cream cheese, or more if desired
2 tablespoons chopped chutney
1 tablespoon curry powder
½ teaspoon dry mustard
¾ cup chopped almonds
Fresh parsley leaves, chopped

Combine the chicken, mayonnaise, cream cheese, chutney, curry powder, dry mustard, and almonds in a medium bowl. Form into a ball, and then roll in the chopped parsley. Serve with toasted pita or crackers.

Sun-Dried Tomato Mousse

Serves 10 to 12

2 sticks unsalted butter, softened
16 ounces cream cheese, softened
½ cup sun-dried tomatoes packed in oil, drained and chopped
1 clove garlic, crushed
1 (6 ounce) can tomato paste
1 tablespoon dried basil
2 teaspoons salt
½ teaspoon freshly ground black pepper
Chopped fresh parsley, for garnish (optional)
Pine nuts, toasted for garnish (optional)

Cream the butter in a bowl until very smooth, but not fluffy. Add the cream cheese and mix until just blended. Stir in the sun-dried tomatoes, garlic, tomato paste, basil, salt, and pepper, being careful not to overmix. Spoon the mixture into a 6-inch springform pan. Cover and chill for 8 hours, or until very firm. Place the pan in hot water for 15 seconds. Release the spring and invert the mousse onto a serving plate. Smooth the top with a warm spatula. Garnish by pressing the parsley or pine nuts onto the sides. Serve with breadsticks or crackers.

Pistachio and Goat Cheese Log
Serves 10 to 12

3 tablespoons finely chopped fresh chives
3 tablespoons finely chopped fresh parsley leaves
¼ teaspoon minced lemon zest
6 ounces cream cheese, chilled
6 ounces goat cheese, such as Montrachet
Salt and freshly ground black pepper to taste
¾ cup shelled, lightly salted pistachios, finely chopped (about 6 ounces unshelled)

Combine the chives, parsley, and lemon zest in small bowl. Place the cream cheese on the center of 8 x 14-inch sheet of plastic wrap. Flatten or shape into a 4 x 6-inch rectangle. Spread with the goat cheese. Cover with another 8 x 14-inch sheet of plastic wrap. Roll out into 6 x 10-inch rectangle. Peel off the top sheet of plastic. Sprinkle the cheese with the parsley mixture, and then season with salt and a generous amount of pepper. Starting from the long side, roll up the cheese tightly in a jelly roll fashion, using the plastic wrap as an aid. Roll the log in the pistachio bits, covering completely. Wrap the log in foil and refrigerate until firm, about 2 hours. After the log has set, unwrap, cut in half crosswise, and trim the ends. Wrap each half tightly in plastic wrap. Refrigerate until ready to serve. (The logs can be prepared up to 1 week ahead.)

Curried Cream Cheese Disc with Chutney
Serves 8

8 ounces cream cheese, softened
½ cup shredded sharp Cheddar cheese
½ teaspoon curry powder
½ jar mango chutney
Grated coconut, for garnish
Chopped pecans, for garnish

Combine the cream cheese, Cheddar cheese, and curry powder in a food processor or with a mixer until well blended. Place the mixture between 2 pieces of wax paper, and pat into a disk approximately ½ inch thick and 6 inches in diameter. Wrap with plastic wrap and refrigerate at least 4 hours.

To serve, transfer the disc to a serving platter and top with the chutney. Sprinkle with coconut and pecans as desired, and serve with water crackers.

Surprise is important.
~ George Balanchine

*Delaware was
named for Thomas West,
Baron De la Warr, the
British colonial governor
of Virginia who never even
saw the state or river that
bear his name. In 1609
Henry Hudson, sailing
for Holland, discovered
Delaware as he explored the
Delaware Bay region in search
of the Northwest Passage.
The following year, Sir Samuel
Argall, sailing on De la Warr's
behalf, took refuge in the bay
and named it after De la Warr.
Just to complicate things
further, the Swedes were the
first to establish a permanent
colony in what is now Delaware.
But the baron's name
remained.*

Pesto and Sun-Dried Tomato Torte

Serves 15

¼ pound provolone cheese, thinly sliced
1 pound cream cheese
2 cloves garlic, minced
1½ teaspoons dried thyme
¼ cup pesto
½ cup sun-dried tomatoes packed in oil, drained and chopped
Additional sun-dried tomatoes, chopped for garnish (optional)
Pine nuts, toasted for garnish (optional)

Line a 9 x 5-inch loaf pan with plastic wrap, leaving several inches overhanging on each side. Place a thin layer of provolone on the bottom and partially up the sides. Place the cream cheese, garlic, and thyme in a food processor and process until smooth. Spread one third of the cream cheese mixture over the provolone. (For easier spreading, dampen the back of a metal spoon with water.) Spread the cream cheese with the pesto. Top the pesto with another third of the cream cheese mixture. Top with the sun-dried tomatoes. Spread the tomatoes with the final third of the cream cheese mixture. Cover with the overlapping plastic wrap and pat down firmly. Chill overnight, or up to 2 days. To serve, invert onto a platter and top with additional chopped sun-dried tomatoes or toasted pine nuts. Serve with crackers or toasted croustades.

Cheese

~ When preparing a cheese board, it is important to select cheeses that complement one another in color and flavor.

~ It is helpful to have more than one cheese knife on hand, especially if you are serving soft cheeses that will stick to the knife.

~ For a more imaginative presentation, try serving your cheese on a marble slab, ceramic tiles, or wicker mats instead of the traditional wooden board. Decorate with fresh herbs, edible flowers such as monarda (bee balm) or nasturtiums, pretty salad leaves, summer berries, and nuts.

~ Invite some friends to taste cheeses from around the world. Compare the various cheeses from a single country, then choose your favorites for an international mix.

Best-Ever Cheese Ring
Serves 10 to 12

1 pound sharp Cheddar cheese, grated
1 cup pecans, chopped
¾ cup mayonnaise
1 medium onion, finely chopped
1 clove garlic, minced
½ teaspoon Tabasco sauce
1 cup strawberry preserves

Combine the cheese, pecans, mayonnaise, onion, garlic, and
Tabasco in a medium bowl; mix well. Invert a small bowl or wide
glass in the center of a serving platter. Mold the cheese mixture
around the bowl and gently cover with plastic wrap. Refrigerator
for 2 to 3 hours to chill. Remove the interior bowl to create a hole in
the ring and fill the hole with the preserves. Serve with crackers.

Party Brie Wheel
Serves 40

1 whole wheel Brie cheese, about 5 pounds
1 cup dried currants
1 cup finely chopped walnuts
1 cup chopped fresh dill leaves
½ cup poppy seeds
1⅓ cups slivered blanched almonds

Remove the rind from the top of the Brie. For easier removal, chill
the Brie first, and then use a sharp knife to remove the top. Lightly
score the top to divide it into 10 wedges, as for a pizza or a pie.
Sprinkle half of the currants on 1 of the wedges. Sprinkle the
remaining currants onto the opposite wedge. Repeat this process
with the remaining ingredients: sprinkle half of the walnuts on one
wedge; the remaining half on the opposite side. Continue with the
dill, poppy seeds, and almonds. Press the ingredients lightly into
the cheese. Then wrap in plastic wrap and chill. Two hours before
serving, remove the Brie from the refrigerator and let come to
room temperature. Place the Brie on a serving plate and surround
with a variety of crackers.

Hors d'oeuvres
by the Dozen

*Handcrafted hors d'oeuvres
are wonderful for intimate
gatherings, but aren't always
practical when serving a
crowd. When you need to
whip up a large batch of hors
d'oeuvres, mini-muffin tins
are the answer. You can use
them to turn quiche, frittatas,
corn bread, and many other
foods into bite-sized portions.
You can double or triple your
favorite recipes; chop the
fillings extra-fine, and bake
⅓-½ as long as you normally
would ~ 10 to 12 minutes
is enough for most
recipes.*

*Alcohol
equivalents:*

*One liter = 33.8 oz. =
twenty-two (22) mixed
drinks (1½ ounces alcohol
in each)*

*One 750 ml bottle of wine =
6 (4-ounce) glasses*

*One 1½ liter bottle of wine =
12 (4-ounce) glasses*

*One bottle of champagne =
6 flute or 7 saucer glasses*

*One case of champagne =
72 drinks*

Brie with Bourbon

Serves 10 to 12

½ cup packed light brown sugar
½ cup chopped pecans
1 to 2 shots of bourbon
1 large wedge Brie, room temperature

Combine the sugar, nuts, and bourbon in a small, microwave-safe bowl. Place the Brie on a microwave-safe serving dish. Microwave the mixture on high for 90 seconds. Stir the mixture to combine, and then pour over the wedge of Brie. Microwave the Brie on high for 30 to 45 seconds. Serve warm with crackers or sliced French bread.

Haag - Vais

Serves 10 to 12

1 (8 ounce) container fat-free cream cheese
½ cup pecans, cashew pieces, or sunflower seeds, toasted
¼ cup jalapeño jelly
½ cup cocktail sauce

Place the cream cheese block on a serving plate and top with the nuts or seeds. Combine the jelly and cocktail sauce in a small bowl, and pour over the cream cheese. Serve with crackers or crudités.

Hot Onion Soufflé

Yields about 6 cups

12 to 16 ounces frozen chopped onions, thawed
24 ounces cream cheese, softened
2 cups freshly grated Parmesan cheese
½ cup mayonnaise

Preheat the oven to 425°F. Roll the thawed onion in paper towels, squeezing to remove any excess moisture. Combine the onions, cream cheese, Parmesan Cheese, and mayonnaise, stirring well. Transfer to a shallow 2-quart soufflé dish. Bake 15 minutes, or until slightly golden brown. Serve with the corn chips or assorted crackers.

Delaware Crab Delight

Serves 10 to 12

1 (8 ounce) package cream cheese, softened with 1 tablespoon milk
10 ounces crabmeat, shelled and picked through
2 tablespoons minced Vidalia onion
1 tablespoon horseradish
¼ teaspoon salt
⅛ teaspoon pepper
⅓ cup sliced almonds
¼ cup mayonnaise, such as Miracle Whip
1½ to 3 tablespoons cream sherry

Preheat the oven to 325°F. Combine all the ingredients in a medium casserole dish. (If planning to serve cold, use 1½ tablespoons of cream sherry; if planning to serve warm, use 3 tablespoons.) Bake for 25 minutes, or until heated through. Serve hot in a chafing dish or refrigerate to chill. Serve with butter or wheat crackers.

Those who bring sunshine to the lives of others cannot keep it from themselves.
~ James M. Barrie

~

To keep celery fresh for a couple of weeks, wash and trim stalks to fit in a gallon-sized ziplock bag. Add ½ to 1 inch of cold water and refrigerate.

Parmesan-Pecan Medley on Cucumber Rounds

Serves 6 to 8

½ cup diced Parmesan cheese
½ cup diced celery
½ cup chopped pecans
Juice of ½ lemon
2 tablespoons mayonnaise
1 clove garlic, pressed
1 hothouse cucumber

Combine the Parmesan, celery, and pecans in a medium bowl. Add the lemon juice, mayonnaise, and pressed garlic, tossing gently to coat. Refrigerate for at least 2 hours, preferably longer to allow the flavors to meld.

While the topping is chilling, slice the cucumber into disks and place between paper towels. Allow to drain for at least hour before assembly. Top each cucumber disk with 1 teaspoon of the medley. Alternatively, serve the Parmesan-pecan medley on endive leaves or wheat crackers. The topping can be stored in an airtight container in the refrigerator for up 2 weeks.

The historic seaport of Lewes, (pronounced Loo-iss), Delaware has among the richest histories of any location in the U.S. It was discovered by Henry Hudson on a voyage up the Delaware River in August 1609, and first settled by the Dutch in 1631. The First Town in the First State, Lewes boasts old homes and structures that date back to the late 1600s and early 1700s. It was also the scene of historic battles, and has been visited by infamous pirates such as Captain Kidd.

Pecan-Crusted Artichoke and Cheese Spread

Yields 15 to 20 appetizer servings

¼ cup butter, divided
1 medium onion, diced
2 cloves garlic, minced
1 (10 ounce) box frozen chopped spinach, thawed and drained
1 (13¾ ounce) can artichoke hearts, drained and chopped
1 (8 ounce) package cream cheese, diced
½ cup mayonnaise
¾ cup (3 ounces) fancy supreme shredded Parmesan cheese
1 (8 ounce) package shredded 4-cheese blend
⅔ cup chopped pecans
½ cup herb-seasoned stuffing mix

Preheat the oven to 350°F. Grease a 2-quart baking dish. Heat a large sauté pan on medium-high and add 3 tablespoons of the butter. Sauté the onion and garlic until tender. Add the spinach, reduce the heat to medium, and cook about 3 minutes, stirring often. Add the artichoke hearts, cream cheeses, mayonnaise, Parmesan, and shredded cheese, stirring until the cheese melts.

Spoon the mixture into the baking dish, and bake for 20 minutes. Combine the remaining tablespoon of butter with the pecans and stuffing mix, and toss until combined well. Sprinkle the topping over the casserole, and bake an additional 15 minutes. Serve with pita chips or French toast.

———

Cooking with Cheese

The secret to cooking with cheese is not to overcook it. Whenever possible, cook it slowly or add it toward the end of the cooking time. Over a certain temperature, the protein (casein) in the cheese coagulates and separates out to form a tough, stringy mass. This is less likely to occur if the cheese is mixed with a starchy food such as flour or bread crumbs. Hard, well-ripened cheeses can tolerate higher temperatures than soft cheese. Fondue, which is kept bubbling at the table, works because the alcohol used to flavor the dish keeps the temperature of the cheese below the point at which it would curdle. Shredding or cutting the cheese into small pieces makes it easier to incorporate. Remember also that the flavor of some cheeses, such as blue cheese, intensifies with heat; goat cheese, on the other hand, loses some of its characteristic mustiness when cooked.

Herbed Cherry Tomatoes and Snow Peas

Serves 10 to 12

1 (8 ounce) package cream cheese, softened
1 to 2 cloves garlic, minced
¼ teaspoon dried basil, or more to taste
¼ teaspoon dried oregano, or more to taste
Salt and freshly ground black pepper to taste
1 package cherry tomatoes, seeded and halved
30 snow peas, seeded and split

Combine the cream cheese, garlic, basil, and oregano. Season with salt and pepper. Spoon into a pastry bag. (If you don't have a pastry bag handy, use a plastic zipperlock bag. Push the cheese mixture to a bottom corner and snip off the corner tip.) Arrange the tomatoes and snow peas cut-side up on a baking sheet. Point the tip of the bag into the center of each tomato and gently squeeze a portion of the cheese mixture into the cavity. For the snow peas, squeeze the bag at an angle to fill the length of the pod. Chill in the refrigerator for 1 to 2 hours before serving.

♪ *The red and green colors of this dish make for a perfect Christmas party appetizer.*

A host is like a general: It takes a mishap to reveal his genius.
~ Horace

Suggested Cheese Boards

Classic French Tasting Board: Comté, Brie de Meaux, Chèvre Log, Pont l'Evêque, Roquefort.

Adventurous French Tasting Board: Bleu d'Auvergne, Valency, Explorateur, Epoisse, Tomme de Savoie, Banon.

Swiss Tasting Board: Appenzell, Emmental, Sapsago, Tête de Moine, Vacherin Mont d'Or.

Italian Tasting Board: Fontina d'Aosta, Gorgonzola, Parmigiano-Reggiano, Robiola, Taleggio.

Classic English Tasting Board: Duckett's Caerphilly, Farmhouse Lancashire, Mature Cheddar, Stilton, Wensleydale.

New British Farmhouse Cheese Tasting Board: Cotherstone, Milleens, Ragstone, Sharpham, Ticklemore.

American Cheese Board: Capriole Banon, Maytag Blue, Shelburne Farm's Raw-milk Cheddar, Cella's Bear Flag Dry Jack.

*Freshly ground seeds of
cumin, coriander and fennel
don't just spice up your
cooking, they also cling to
the grinder. For a quick
cleanup, run soft, fresh white
bread through the grinder to
pick up lingering spices and
absorb the oils they leave
behind. This trick works
for coffee grinders, too.*

Lobster and Guacamole
on Seasonal Tortilla

Serves 6 to 12

6 (11 inch) flour tortillas
Seasonal cookie cutter, such as a Christmas star, Valentine heart, etc.
2 ripe avocados, chopped
½ cup diced red onion
2 teaspoons chopped fresh cilantro leaves
1 tablespoon freshly squeezed lime juice
1 plum tomato, seeded and chopped
½ cup sour cream
1 teaspoon ground cumin
⅛ teaspoon cayenne pepper
1 pound cooked lobster meat, cut into small portions and chilled

Preheat the oven to 300°F. Press the cookie cutter into each tortilla.
Bake the cut tortillas on a cookie sheet for 10 to 12 minutes.
Reserve in an airtight container.

To prepare the guacamole, combine the avocados, red onion,
cilantro, lime juice, and tomato. Cover with plastic wrap, pressing
the wrap directly onto the guacamole to prevent oxidation and
help keep it green. (The guacamole can be made several hours
ahead and refrigerated.)

To prepare the spicy sour cream, blend together the sour cream,
cumin, and cayenne in a small bowl.

To serve, place the cut out tortillas on a tray. Top with a dollop of
guacamole. Place 1 piece of lobster on top of the guacamole.
Garnish with the spicy sour cream, using a squeeze bottle to
drizzled the mixture over the top. Serve cold.

Appetizers

Marinated Shrimp

Serves 20

5 pounds fresh large shrimp
4 white onions, thinly sliced
2 cups vegetable oil
½ cup cider vinegar
4 ounces capers, brine included
1½ teaspoons salt
1 teaspoon Tabasco sauce
2 tablespoons Worcestershire sauce
2 cups sugar

Boil the shrimp in water to cover until just pink. Shell and devein the cooked shrimp.

Combine the onions, vegetable oil, vinegar, capers and their brine, salt, Tabasco, Worcestershire, and sugar in a large, non-reactive bowl, stirring to help dissolve the sugar. Add the shrimp to the marinade and marinate for at least 2 days, stirring occasionally.

For a beautiful presentation, pile ice in a large silver punch bowl or platter and mound with the shrimp. If using frozen, precooked shrimp, simply add directly to the marinade. It is not necessary to thaw before using.

Count Per Pound:

- *Jumbo shrimp: 11-15 shrimp/lb.*

- *Extra-large shrimp: 16-20/lb.*

- *Large shrimp: 21-30/lb.*

- *Medium shrimp: 31-35/lb.*

- *Small shrimp: 36 or more/lb.*

Burgundy Mushrooms

Makes 4 cups

2 pounds medium-size fresh mushrooms
1⅔ cups Burgundy wine
1 cup beef broth
¼ cup butter or margarine
2 teaspoons Worcestershire sauce
¾ teaspoon salt
½ teaspoon dill seed
½ teaspoon freshly ground black pepper
3 or 4 cloves garlic, minced

Combine all the ingredients in a 4-quart Dutch oven and bring to a boil. Reduce the heat, cover, and simmer for 1 hour. Uncover and simmer for 2 more hours, or until only a small amount of liquid remains. Transfer to a 1½ or 2-quart chafing dish and serve hot as an hors d'oeuvre or as a garnish for grilled steaks.

*Peter Minuit
(best known for purchasing
the island of Manhattan
from Native Americans a
decade earlier), guided two
ships, the Kalmar Nyckel and
Vogle Grip, up the Delaware
Bay in 1638. On a ledge of
rocks that survives today, the
settlers stepped ashore. They
built a fort nearby and named
it, along with the river, for
the 12 year old queen of
Sweden: Christina.*

Feta Shrimp Triangles
Makes 40 triangles

4 pita pockets
6 ounces feta cheese
8 ounces shrimp, peeled, deveined, and chopped
2 cloves garlic, minced
½ cup mayonnaise
½ teaspoon chili powder
½ teaspoon ground cumin
2 tablespoons chopped fresh mint leaves
Sesame seeds, for garnish
Paprika, for garnish

Preheat the oven to 300°F. Split the pitas and cut into triangles. Bake for 15 to 20 minutes, or until lightly browned. Preheat the broiler. Crumble the feta over the triangles. Combine the shrimp, garlic, mayonnaise, chili powder, cumin, and mint. Spread over the feta. Sprinkle with the sesame seeds and paprika. Broil until browned and bubbly. Serve immediately.

Cheese Storage

Cover prepared cheese boards with plastic wrap, aluminum foil, or a glass dome; the cheese will remain fresh for an hour or two at room temperature. For longer periods, add a sugar cube to absorb the moisture that will evaporate from the cheese. Protect cheese by wrapping it in aluminum foil or wax paper, or place in a plastic box with a tight-fitting lid. These methods allow the cheese to breath. Plastic wrap is useful only for very short-term storage; if left too long, the rind will become slimy and the paste may sweat. For soft cheeses, make sure the wrapping is pressed against the cut side of the cheese, which will help keep it from running. Wrap each cheese individually, so that their flavors do not mingle. Store cheese in the warmest sections of the refrigerator, such as the door or the salad crisper. Storage time varies with the type of cheese; soft cheeses do not keep well, but semi-hard and hard cheeses, such as Emmental or Parmesan, can be kept for several weeks. If you buy a large piece, cut it into smaller pieces before storing so that you do not need to bring the entire cheese to room temperature before use. Freezing cheese is not recommended, as soft cheeses lose their flavor and hard cheeses will get crumbly.

Traditional Saté

Serves a crowd

Marinade and Meats

1 cup low-salt teriyaki sauce
4 cloves garlic, minced
3 tablespoons freshly squeezed lime juice
2½ tablespoons peeled and minced fresh ginger
2 tablespoons packed light brown sugar
24 medium-size uncooked shrimp, peeled and deveined
1¼ pounds boneless chicken breasts, cut into ½-inch-wide strips
1¼ pounds filet mignon, cut into ½-inch-wide strips
40 wooden skewers, soaked in water 30 minutes

Dipping Sauce

1 cup creamy peanut butter
1 (14½ ounce) can low-salt chicken broth
¼ cup freshly squeezed lime juice
3 tablespoons packed dark brown sugar
2 tablespoons plus 1 teaspoon low-salt soy sauce
2 tablespoons peeled and chopped fresh ginger
½ teaspoon crushed red pepper flakes
1 lime, sliced into rounds or wedges, for garnish

Combine the teriyaki sauce, garlic, lime juice, minced ginger and brown sugar in large glass baking dish, stirring until the sugar dissolves. Add the shrimp, chicken, and beef, and stir to coat. Cover and chill for 30 minutes to 1 hour.

To prepare the dipping sauce, place the peanut butter in a medium saucepan over medium heat. Gradually stir in the chicken broth, lime juice, brown sugar, soy sauce, chopped ginger, and red pepper. Continue to stir over medium heat until smooth and thick, about 6 minutes

Pour the dipping sauce into a serving bowl and garnish with fresh lime rounds or wedges.

Prepare the grill to a medium-high heat or preheat the broiler.

Remove the shrimp, chicken, and beef from the marinade. Thread onto separate skewers, using about 3 shrimp, 2 beef strips, and 2 chicken pieces per skewer. Each skewer should be arranged as follows: shrimp, beef, chicken, shrimp, chicken, beef, shrimp.

Grill the skewered meats until the chicken and shrimp are cooked through, about 3 minutes per side. Serve with the peanut sauce.

America's newest tall ship, ten stories high and 139 feet long, is a recreation of the Kalmar Nyckel, which landed on the Christina River in 1638. Visitors can tour the ship at The Kalmar Nyckel Shipyard in Wilmington, a living-history museum, featuring cultural, historical and educational programs emphasizing the rich maritime heritage of Delaware.

Try this trick for opening a stubborn jar lid: Place one wide rubber band around the lid and another around the jar. Grip each band, and twist the lid open.

~

Do your hands burn when chopping chilies? Capsaicin, the chemical that gives chilies their heat, is mostly contained in the ribs, veins and seeds of the chili; it is also in the flesh, but at much lower levels. To prevent burning, rub your hands with vinegar as soon as you are finished, or rinse them with rubbing alcohol to help break down the capsaicin, then wash them thoroughly with soap and water.

Mexican Egg Rolls with Spicy Guacamole Dipping Sauce

Serves 8

Guacamole Dipping Sauce

1 avocado, peeled, seeded, and coarsely chopped
1 cup sour cream
½ cup medium-hot picante sauce
⅓ cup finely chopped fresh cilantro leaves
1 tablespoon grated onion
1 (4 ounce) can chopped green chiles

Egg Rolls

2 tablespoons vegetable oil
1½ pounds chicken breast, cut into ½-inch pieces
2½ cups finely chopped onion
1 to 2 tablespoons dry chili mix, to taste
1 cup drained and rinsed canned black beans
1 (4 ounce) can chopped green chiles
2 cups grated Mexican blend cheeses
½ cup finely chopped fresh cilantro leaves
½ jalapeño pepper, seeded and chopped (optional)
3 tablespoons picante sauce
1 teaspoon salt
1 pound egg roll wrappers (16 wrappers)

To prepare the dipping sauce, combine all the ingredients in a food processor and blend until combined. Chill until ready to serve.

To prepare the egg rolls, heat the oil in a large frying pan on medium-high. Add the chicken and onions, and sauté for several minutes. Stir in the chili mix, and continue cooking until the onions turn translucent and the chicken is cooked through. Remove the pan from the heat, and stir in the beans, chiles, cheese, cilantro, jalapeño, picante sauce, and salt.

On a lightly floured surface, spoon ¼ of the chicken filling onto a single egg roll wrapper. Follow the package directions to roll up into an egg roll. Repeat for the remaining wrappers. (The rolls can be refrigerated for 1 day or frozen for 1 week at this point.)

In a wide frying pan, fill enough vegetable oil to come ½ inch up the sides and heat to 370°F. Carefully place 2 to 3 egg rolls in at the time, frying about 3 minutes per side. (Be sure to wait between

Mexican Egg Rolls with Spicy Guacamole Dipping Sauce, continued

batches for the oil to return to 370°F.) Drain on paper towels and serve immediately with the dipping sauce. If not serving immediately, refrigerate and then reheat for 20 minutes at 350°F.

Hot Goat Cheese and Raisin Brioche

Serves 2 to 4

4 (4 to 5 inch) brioches, halved
4 Crottin de Charignol (a hard, dry, round French goat cheese), halved, or 1 log Montrachet or Bucheron, sliced into rounds.
⅓ cup raisins
3 tablespoons cognac
1¾ cups dry red wine
¾ cup port
1 stick unsalted butter, sliced into tablespoons and chilled
Salt and freshly ground black pepper to taste

Preheat the oven to 425°F. Arrange the brioche halves, cut-side up, on a baking sheet. Top each half with a piece of cheese. Bake until the cheese is soft, about 12 to 14 minutes. Combine the raisins and cognac in small, heavy skillet over medium-high heat. Tilt the pan, warm the cognac, and ignite. When the flames have subsided, add the red wine and port, and bring to a boil. When reduced to ¼ cup, remove from the heat. Whisk in the chilled butter, 1 tablespoon at a time, until fully incorporated. Season with salt and pepper. Spoon the sauce onto serving plates. Arrange 2 brioche halves on each plate and serve immediately.

The literal meaning of the original French phrase hors d'oeuvre is "outside the work," an architectural term referring to an outbuilding not incorporated into the architect's main design. The phrase was borrowed by France's culinary experts to indicate appetizers, which are customarily served apart from the main course of a dinner. Thus hors d'oeuvres are, quite literally, outside the main design of the meal.

A diamond is a chunk of coal that made good under pressure.

~ Anonymous

Gougères

Makes about 20 puffs

1 cup milk
1 stick (8 tablespoons) unsalted butter
1 teaspoon salt
1 cup sifted, unbleached, all-purpose flour
5 eggs, divided
1½ cups freshly grated Parmesan cheese (or half Parmesan, half Gruyère), plus ½ cup freshly grated Parmesan to top puffs (optional)

Combine the milk, butter, and salt in a small, heavy saucepan, and bring to a boil. Remove the pan from the heat and add the flour all at once. Whisk vigorously for a few moments, and then return the pan to medium heat. Cook, stirring constantly, until the batter has thickened and is pulling away from the sides and bottom of the pan-about 5 minutes or less.

Remove the pan from the heat and beat in 4 of the eggs with a wooden spoon, one at a time, making certain that each egg is thoroughly incorporated before adding the next. Stir in 1½ cups of the cheese.

Preheat the oven to 375°F. Lightly butter a baking sheet.

Drop the batter by tablespoonfuls onto the baking sheet, spacing the puffs at least 1 inch apart. Beat the remaining egg in a small bowl. Brush the tops of the puffs with the beaten egg and sprinkle with the additional Parmesan, if desired. (The egg wash will produce a crusty top. For a softer, lighter-colored top, omit the egg wash.)

Set the baking sheet on the center rack of the oven and immediately reduce the heat to 350°F. Bake for 15 to 20 minutes, or until the gougères are puffed and browned. Serve immediately.

These Gougères can be made ahead of time. Simply bake the puffs, cool on wire racks, wrap in plastic bags, and freeze. To serve, remove from the freezer and allow to thaw at least partially. Preheat the oven to 200°F. to 300°F. Place the puffs on a baking sheet or stone and reheat for 10 to 20 minutes, depending on their size.

♪ *These cheese puffs work well in many different sizes. For perfect party fare, make teaspoon-size, pop-in-your-mouth puffs. For a spicy effect, substitute Cheddar cheese for the Parmesan and add diced jalapeño peppers. Sprinkle with paprika and bake as usual.*

Authentic Buffalo Wings
Serves 12

Chicken Wings

1 (4 pound) bag chicken wings (about 48 wings)
Canola oil, for deep frying

Sauce

1½ cups Frank's Red Hot Sauce
½ stick unsalted butter
½ teaspoon celery salt or garlic salt

To prepare the chicken, cut the wings at the joints. Reserve the tips for stock or discard. Rinse the wings thoroughly. Arrange on several layers of paper towels and top with additional layers. Pat to dry thoroughly.

Pour enough canola oil to come ⅓ up the sides of a large, deep pot and set over high heat. The oil needs to reach 375°F. to 400°F. for proper frying.

While the oil is heating, prepare the sauce. Combine the hot sauce, butter, and celery or garlic salt in a small saucepan over medium heat until the butter is melted. Reduce the heat to low to keep the sauce warm until ready to serve.

When the oil has reached at least 375°F., carefully place 12 to 20 wings in the oil. After 5 to 8 minutes, the wings will float to the surface. Continue to fry the wings an additional 5 to 8 minutes to insure thorough cooking. (Total cooking time will vary, but 12 to 15 minutes usually produces a moist, crispy product.)

Remove the wings with a slotted spoon, shaking to drip off excess oil, and place in a large bowl. Let wings stand 1 or 2 minutes, then drizzle in 2 to 3 tablespoons of the warm sauce, or more to taste. Toss the sauce with the wings until coated thoroughly.

Continue frying the chicken in batches, being careful to wait until the temperature of the oil has again reached 375°F. before adding more wings.

♪ *Wings that are fried ahead of time and then reheated or kept warm in the oven produce lackluster results. So, for large groups, it works best to prepare the wings in batches and serve immediately.*

Though called New Sweden, the first Delaware colony, established at Fort Christina in 1638, was also home to many Finns. These hardy settlers had once carved farms from Sweden's remote forests. Now in Delaware, they continued to build their homes from logs, bringing to the New World one of the enduring symbols of the American pioneer, the log cabin. One of these cabins has been preserved, and is on display at the Delaware Agricultural Museum in Dover.

Cheeses

Cheese	Region	Style	Taste/Texture
Asiago d'allevo	Italy	Hard	Nutty with lemony aftertaste. Pale straw-colored, supple but sliceable, many small holes.
Boursin (Rondelé and Alouette are American brand names for similar cheese spreads)	Normandy	Soft	Savory, flavored with garlic & herbs.
Cantal	Auvergne, France	Semi-hard	Milky aroma, nutty flavor with attractive lingering acidity. Pale yellow, close textured and smooth.
Comté	N.E. France	Hard	Wonderful floral aroma with nutty fudge flavors and a salty finish. Dark straw-colored, with medium-sized holes; tends to crack on cutting.
Epoisse	N.W. France	Soft	Soft and supple, with very strong farmyard-like flavor and sharp, tangy aroma. Rustic, but creamy and refreshing, with sour lemon aftertaste.
Fontina	N.W. Italy	Semi-hard	Smooth and buttery, almost spreadable, when young. Pale straw color with a few small holes. Gets darker and much drier with age. Starts milky and lightly scented from alpine meadows; older cheese has earthy but fruity aroma with mellow flavor of nuts and fruit.
Gorgonzola	N. Italy	Semi-hard blue-veined	White to pale yellow, with good spread of greenish-blue veins. Texture quite creamy; moister than Stilton and more buttery than Roquefort.

Cheeses

Pungency	Uses	Wine
Medium-strong	Serve younger cheese with Italian bread. Shred older cheese over pasta or soup, or stir into risottos.	Chardonnay
Mild-medium	Serve with fresh baguettes, crispbread or pumpernickel. Use as canapé topping, or for stuffing celery, dates or tomatoes.	Sancerre or Sauvignon Blanc
Mild	Serve with country-style bread and fresh fruit. Shreds and melts well; very useful in cooking.	Rioja
Mild	Serve after dinner with fruit, or use in sandwiches with cold ham or salami.	Chianti Classico Riserva or Rioja
One of top 10 most pungent French cheeses.	Best served on its own with plain water biscuits or a fresh baguette, rather than used in cooking, due to strong flavor.	Mature red burgundy
Mild	Serve with celery or grapes, or use in toasted sandwiches. Marvelous for cooking.	Barbaresco or Recioto della Valpolicella
Strong	Serve on cheese board.	Barolo or Reciota della Valpolicella

Cheeses

Cheese	Region	Style	Taste/Texture
Mahon	Spain	Semi-hard to hard	Distinctively fruity, ivory cheese that darkens and hardens as it ages, developing a scattering of tiny holes. Sweet, floral aroma, but taste is surprisingly sour and slightly tangy with roasted nuts and fudgy toffee aftertastes.
Pont l'Evêque	N.W. France	Soft	Distinctive square shape. Yellow paste is supple, with a few small holes. Rind has farmyard aroma, with bacon and ammonia. Paste has much milder aroma reminiscent of nuts. Flavor is mild and sweet.
Port Salut	N.E. France	Semi-soft	Smooth, springy yellow paste. Aroma and flavor very mild, with hint of earthy nuttiness.
Raclette	Switzerland	Semi-hard	Dark ivory to yellow. Very smooth, seems to melt in the mouth even without heating. Aroma strongly reminiscent of stableyard with fruit and wine. Taste is equally strong, with winelike notes and a tangy accent.
Reblochon	N.E. France	Soft	Pinkish-gray rind; paste is very supple, with a number of small holes. Fairly pungent aroma, but flavor is mild, fruity and creamy.
Stilton	Central England	Semi-hard blue	Paste is crumbly when young, softening and darkening at the rind as it matures. Creamy ivory with well-spread blue veining growing from the center outward. Veining increases and turns bright blue-green with age. Aroma sharply nutty and flavor full of mellow nuts and fruit; strengthens as it matures.

Cheeses

Pungency	Uses	Wine
Medium	Serve on cheese board or in sandwiches, or serve it as they do in Spain: Sliced, sprinkled with olive oil, salt and fresh tarragon.	Red Rioja
Pungent	Serve as cheese course with grapes and water biscuits. In cooking, it goes well with potatoes.	Rioja Reserva or Calvados
Mild	Easy-eating cheese. Serve in chunks with fruit or raw vegetables. Slice or melt for use in sandwiches.	Bergerac or Valpolicella
Strong	Not usually served uncooked in Switzerland, but very good sliced and served with airdried ham. When cooked, Raclette melts to a velvety mass.	Beaujolais
Medium	Serve as cheese course with celery or radishes. Can also be deep fried in breadcrumbs and served with homemade fruit chutney.	Claret
Strong	Good after-dinner cheese.	Port

Cheeses

Cheese	Region	Style	Taste/Texture
Taleggio	N. Italy	Semi-soft	Deep pinkish-orange washed rind, with supple, pale ivory paste. Exotic aroma of raisins, nuts, and tangy lemons, with farmyard-like tones. Melts in the mouth with a beautiful full fruity taste.
Tilsit	Germany	Semi-hard	Springy and elastic but fairly moist. Some are mild and lightly tangy, but the better cheeses have a big spicy taste.
Tomme de Savoie	N. E. France	Semi-hard	Rustic appearance. Pale ivory, darkening at the rind, and supple, with few small holes. Aroma strongly grassy with ammonia, mushrooms and caramel tones. Flavor is much sweeter, with a fudge taste and a citrus tang.
Wensleydale	N.E. England	Hard	Rind is dry, pale yellow; paste is pretty pale primrose color, firm but crumbly. Aroma is fragrantly sweet and milky, with grassy note. Taste is similar, with a citrus tang that sharpens to tart apples and attractive lemony aftertaste.

From The Cheese Companion: The Connoisseur's Guide by Judy Ridgway.
Running Press, Philadelphia * London, 1999

Cheeses

Pungency	Uses	Wine
Medium	Serve Taleggio as the star of the cheese course with walnut bread and a fruit bowl. Or serve as a snack with bitter salad leaves and very ripe tomatoes. Melts well, and is excellent sliced over polenta or mixed into risotto. Use on bruschetta with roasted zucchini and sage. Factory-produced Taleggio is whiter and milder than a good farmhouse version.	Chianti Classico Riserva or Recioto de Soave
Medium	Versatile cheese. Germans serve it thin-sliced for breakfast, cut into chunks in salads and for snacks, or in large wedges on a cheese board after dinner. It toasts well, and makes an excellent topping for hamburgers. Also good for cooking, melted into cheese sauces for pasta and potato dishes.	German Beer
Mild-medium	Beware of Tomme de Savoie look-alikes, which have a smooth rind and boring taste. Look for the words "fabrique en Savoie" rather than "affiné de Savoie" on authentic cheeses. Serve with bread and salad or fruit. Also good for toasting.	Beaujolais
Medium	Fruitcake, gingerbread, and apple pie are the traditional accompaniments to Wensleydale cheese. However, it goes equally well with bread and crackers, or with fresh fruit such as pears and grapes. Eat as soon after purchase as possible. Cooks very well. Also comes in smoked and blue versions.	Chardonnay

Notes

**Above: Farmhouse Kitchen,
Agricultural Museum**

Right: Nemours Kitchen

Do the Twist
Beverages, Bread & Breakfast

Farmhouse Kitchen, Agricultural Museum

The Delaware Agricultural Museum and Village in Dover, is dedicated to the history and technology of farm life and culture in Delaware and on the Delmarva Peninsula. This photo features the summer kitchen of the farmhouse, where three meals a day were prepared from scratch, food was preserved for use during the winter, and the family's clothing was cared for.

Photograph by Kevin Fleming, courtesy of the Delaware Tourism Office, Delaware Economic Development Office

Nemours Kitchen

The Nemours Mansion, built in 1909, is set among spectacular French formal gardens. The Louis XVI-style château was built for Alfred I. du Pont, and contains 102 rooms furnished with fine examples of antique furniture, rare rugs, tapestries and outstanding works of art dating back to the 15th century. An intimate guided tour through rooms on three floors, and a bus tour through the recently refurbished French-inspired gardens, concludes with a visit to the chauffeur's garage, where the family's antique cars may be seen.

Pictured here is a wicker basket, on one of the worktables in the kitchen. It was made in London for B. Altman, New York, and is monogrammed "DP" on the top. It is fully outfitted with plates and utensils with leather straps, serving pieces, and glasses with wicker sleeves.

Photograph courtesy of The Nemours Foundation

Brandy Slush Punch

Serves 8 to 10

1 (6 ounce) container frozen orange juice concentrate, thawed and undiluted

1 (6 ounce) container frozen lemonade concentrate, thawed and undiluted

1 quart plus ½ to 1 cup water

1 cup apricot brandy

¾ cup sugar

1 quart lemon-lime carbonated beverage, divided

Combine the orange juice concentrate, lemonade concentrate, water, apricot brandy, and sugar in a freezer-safe container, and stir until the sugar dissolves. Freeze for 24 hours. Spoon 3 cups of the frozen mixture into an electric blender. Add 2 cups of lemon-lime beverage. Blend 20 seconds on high speed. Pour into serving glasses and serve immediately.

Friendship Tea

Serves 8

5 tablespoons orange pekoe tea leaves or 1 quart-size orange pekoe tea bag

4 cups boiling water

2 cups freshly squeezed orange juice

½ cup freshly squeezed lemon juice

Sugar to taste

3 cups ginger ale

8 thin orange slices, for garnish

Pour the boiling water over the tea leaves or quart tea bag and steep for 10 minutes. Strain the tea into a pitcher and allow it to cool. When cool, add the orange juice, lemon juice, and sugar. Stir until the sugar dissolves, and then chill the tea. Before serving, add the ginger ale and pour into tall glasses filled with ice. Garnish each drink with one of the orange slices.

Fresh grapes look lovely on the table, but they do tend to wilt there. Freezing seedless grapes not only revives them, it turns them into a cooling treat as well. Rinse grapes under running water and pat dry. Place on a tray and freeze for 2 hours or until firm. Served immediately, grapes are tangy and firm. But even if they defrost a bit, they'll still be delicious.

Peach Iced Tea

Serves 4 to 6

Tea

1 quart-size orange pekoe tea bag
4 cups boiling water
1⅓ cups simple syrup, or more to taste
5 (5½ ounce) cans peach nectar (about 3⅓ cups), chilled

Simple Syrup

1⅓ cups sugar
1¼ cups water
Peach slices, for garnish

For the tea, pour the boiling water over the tea bags and steep for 5 to 10 minutes. Strain the tea into a pitcher and refrigerate until completely chilled.

To prepare the simple syrup, combine the sugar and water in small saucepan and bring to a boil. Stir until the sugar is dissolved, and then continue simmering for about 5 minutes. Let the syrup cool, and then cover and chill until ready to use. (The syrup can be made up to 2 weeks ahead.)

When the tea and simple syrup have chilled, stir the nectar and syrup into the tea, adding more if necessary to taste. Pour the tea into tall glasses filled with ice.

Do you have a decanter that's hard to dry? If you roll a paper towel tightly and insert it three-quarters of the way into the bottle, it will wick away the moisture.

~

A woman is like a tea bag ~ you can't tell how strong she is until you put her in hot water.

~ Nancy Reagan

Classic Mimosa

Fill Champagne flute ¼-full of fresh-squeezed orange juice, then finish filling with Champagne. For an elegant touch, add two dashes of Grand Marnier.

Texas Margaritas

Serves 4 to 6

8 ounces tequila, preferably Especial Jose Cuervo

4 cups margarita mix, preferably Jose Cuervo

3 ounces Cointreau

2 ounces Triple Sec

2 ounces brandy, preferably El Presidente

Lime wedges, for garnish

Margarita salt, for garnish

Combine the tequila, margarita mix, Cointreau, Triple Sec, and brandy in a large pitcher. Chill. (Do not add ice, as it will dilute the flavor.) To serve, rub the rim of a margarita glass with a lime wedge. Dip the edge into the margarita salt. Fill the glass with ice and pour in the chilled margarita mixture.

Sangría Blanca

Serves 8 to 10

½ cup sugar

½ freshly squeezed lemon juice (approximately 4 lemons)

1 (750 ml) bottle dry white wine

½ cup freshly squeezed orange juice

¼ cup orange flavored liqueur

1 lemon, thinly sliced

1 liter club soda

Orange slices, strawberries, fresh pineapple spears, and seedless grapes (optional)

Mint, for garnish

Combine the sugar and lemon juice in a large pitcher, stirring to dissolve the sugar. Add the wine, orange juice, liqueur, lemon slices, and enough ice cubes to chill the mixture. Stir well. Just before serving, add the club soda. Offer fresh fruit as an accompaniment, and garnish with the mint, if desired.

Natural Sake Cups

Cold sake, the Japanese rice wine, is sometimes served in a boxy cup and garnished with a cucumber slice. Try making the cups themselves out of fragrant cucumbers. Japanese cucumbers, with fewer seeds and less pulp, make the tidiest cups. Slice ends off cucumber, then slice crosswise into three 2-inch sections. Stand one section at a time on its base; slice outsides from top to bottom, squaring cucumber; reserve peelings. With apple corer, hollow out centers, leaving ½ inch for bottom of cup. Cut cucumber peelings into matchsticks; dip into sake, and sprinkle with salt to bring out the sake's sweetness. The chilled sake is not meant to be sipped, but downed in a single shot. If you prefer, you can substitute vodka or tequila.

Wine and Champagne Punch

Serves 16

5 Kiwi fruit, peeled and sliced
3 pears, cored and cut into chunks
3 apples, cored and cut into chunks
16 large strawberries, hulled and halved
Block of ice or decorative ice mold
8 (750 ml) bottles Fume Blanc, well chilled
1 (750 ml) bottle Riesling, well chilled
1 (750 ml) bottle Champagne, well chilled
¾ cup pear brandy

Thread the fruit evenly onto 16 (6 inch) bamboo skewers. Place the ice in center of the punch bowl. Add the chilled wine, Champagane and brandy and mix gently. To serve, ladle the punch into goblets and garnish with the skewered fruit.

The 87-foot tall Fenwick Island Lighthouse was painted in 1880 for a total cost of about $5.00.

Beer Bread

Yields 1 loaf

3 cups flour
3 tablespoons sugar
1 bottle or can beer, preferably a brown ale

Preheat the oven to 350°F. Grease a bread pan. Combine all the ingredients well and pour into the bread pan. Bake for 50 to 55 minutes, or until golden brown.

Banana Rum Bread

Yields 1 loaf

4 or 5 bananas
White Rum, for marinating
1 cup sugar
½ cup vegetable oil
2 eggs, beaten
1 teaspoon baking soda
½ teaspoon baking powder
2 cups flour
½ teaspoon salt
¾ tablespoon milk
½ teaspoon pure vanilla extract
1 cup chopped black walnuts

Preheat the oven to 350°F. Mash the bananas in a small bowl. Pour enough rum over the top of them to cover and let set for 2 or 3 days in the refrigerator. After the bananas have soaked, combine the sugar and vegetable oil in a medium bowl. Add the eggs and banana mixture, and beat to mix well. Stir in the baking soda, baking powder, flour, salt, milk, vanilla, and walnuts, combining well. Pour into a standard loaf pan. Bake for 1 hour, or until a knife inserted in the center comes out clean.

Hagley Museum boasts more than 230 acres of great natural beauty along the Brandywine River, featuring mills, millraces, a workers' community, gardens and the first du Pont home in the New World.

~

If you want to lift yourself up, lift up someone else.
~ Booker T. Washington

In 1682, William Penn
first set foot on the shores of
the New World to lay claim
to two huge land grants given
to him by King Charles II
and the Duke of York. There
he accepted a piece of turf and
a porringer of water signifying
the conveyance of these grants,
known as "Pennsylvania"
(Penn's Woodlands) and
"the Lower Counties Upon
Delaware." A second ceremony
took place a few days later
in Cantwell's Bridge,
today the historic town
of Odessa.

One Bowl, No-Knead French Bread

Yields 2 loaves

1 tablespoon yeast
2 cups lukewarm water
4 cups unbleached flour
1 tablespoon sugar
2 teaspoons salt

Dissolve the yeast in 1 cup of the lukewarm water. Sift the flour, sugar, and salt together in a large bowl. Add the yeast to the flour mixture and blend thoroughly. Add just enough of the second cup of lukewarm water to make a soft, sticky dough. Cover with a towel and let rise in a warm, moist spot until doubled in size-about 1½ hours. Punch down. Butter 2 baguette pans very well. Place the dough into the pans and let rise until doubled in size again-another 1 to 1½ hours. Place the pans in a cold oven and bake at 350°F. for about an hour.

Date Bread

Yields 3 loaves

1½ cups water
2 teaspoons baking soda
2 cups chopped dates
1½ cups sugar
2 eggs
1 teaspoon pure vanilla extract
½ teaspoon salt
2½ cups flour

Preheat the oven to 350°F. Bring the water to a boil in medium saucepan. Stir in the baking soda and dates, and then remove from the heat. Blend the sugar, eggs, vanilla, and salt in a medium bowl, mixing well. Add the cooled date mixture, then add the flour in batches until well incorporated. Pour the batter to come halfway up the sides of 3 standard loaf pans or multiple mini loaf pans. Bake 1 hour for standard loaf pans or 45 minutes for mini loaves. Serve with cream cheese.

Carrot Bread

Yields 1 loaf

1½ cups flour
1½ teaspoons baking soda
2 teaspoons baking powder
3 eggs
1 cup sugar
½ cup oil
2 tablespoons hot water
1 cup grated carrots
½ teaspoon cinnamon
½ teaspoon nutmeg
½ teaspoon salt

Preheat the oven to 350°F. Grease a standard loaf pan. Combine the flour, baking soda, and baking powder together in a small bowl. Combine the eggs, sugar, oil, hot water, carrots, cinnamon, nutmeg, and salt in a large bowl; blend well. Stir in the flour mixture and blend well. Pour the batter into the loaf pan and bake for 55 to 60 minutes.

*It is a fine seasoning
for joy, to think of
those we love.*

~ Moliere

Sausage Bread

Good

Yields 1 loaf

1 loaf frozen bread dough, thawed
1 pound hot sausage, browned
1 cup freshly grated Parmesan cheese *— or cheddar*
2 eggs
Butter for glazing, room temperature

Roll out the bread dough to make a large rectangle. Combine the sausage, cheese, and eggs in a small bowl. Spread the mixture onto the dough, and then roll up the dough like a jelly roll. Place seam-side down on a baking sheet. Rub with margarine and bake according to package directions for 35 to 40 minutes. Slice and serve warm.

Lemon-Almond Buttermilk Bread with Balsamic Strawberries

Yields 1 loaf

Balsamic Strawberries

3½ cups sliced strawberries
¼ cup sugar
1½ tablespoons balsamic vinegar

Bread

2¼ cups flour
½ teaspoon salt
½ teaspoon baking soda
1½ cups sugar
1½ sticks unsalted butter, room temperature
3 large eggs
½ teaspoon almond extract
¾ cup buttermilk
¾ cup ground almonds
1 tablespoon grated lemon zest

Lemon Glaze

½ cup sugar
5 tablespoons freshly squeezed lemon juice

To prepare the balsamic strawberries, toss the strawberries, sugar, and balsamic vinegar in bowl. Let stand at room temperature for 1 to 3 hours to let the flavors meld.

To prepare the bread, preheat the oven to 350°F. Butter and flour a standard loaf pan. Sift the flour, salt, and baking soda together into a medium bowl. Cream the sugar with the butter in large bowl using an electric mixer until well blended. Add the eggs one at a time, beating well after each addition. Mix in the almond extract. Add the flour mixture to the egg mixture, alternating with the buttermilk, in 3 batches each. Beat well after each addition. Add the almonds and zest, and beat for another minute. Place the batter in the pan.

Bake the bread until a deep, golden brown, cracked on top, and a knife inserted in the center comes out clean, about 1 hour and 25 minutes. Cool the bread in pan on a rack for 15 minutes before turning out.

Buttermilk Substitute:

Add 1 tablespoon lemon juice or white vinegar to 1 cup whole or low-fat milk. Let mixture stand for several minutes until it begins to curdle, then use for baking. Plain yogurt also works well in salad dressings and dips that call for buttermilk.

~

To remove a stain from the bottom of a glass vase or cruet, fill with water and drop in two Alka-Seltzer tablets.

Lemon-Almond Buttermilk Bread with Balsamic Strawberries, continued

While the bread is cooling, prepare the glaze. Combine the sugar and lemon juice in a small bowl until the sugar dissolves. Place the bread on a serving plate. Poke holes 1 to 2 inches apart all over the bread. Brush the top and sides of bread with the lemon glaze, allowing some to soak into the bread before brushing with more. Serve with the Balsamic Strawberries.

Sweet Potato Biscuits

Yields 20 biscuits

1 pound sweet potatoes, peeled and cubed into 2-inch pieces
4 cups all-purpose flour
½ cup packed light brown sugar
5 teaspoons baking powder
1 teaspoon salt
10 tablespoons butter
⅓ cup milk

Boil the potatoes until tender, about 12 to 15 minutes. Drain, mash, and set aside to cool. Preheat the oven to 425°F. Combine the flour, sugar, baking powder, and salt. Cut in the butter with a pastry blender until you have pea-size pieces. Stir in the milk and mashed potatoes, mixing just until combined. Pat the dough into an 8½-inch square on a lightly floured surface. Cut the dough in half. Cut each half into 10 equal pieces. Place the biscuits 2 inches apart on 2 ungreased cookie sheets. Bake 12 to 15 minutes; the biscuit bottoms should not turn brown.

♪ *This recipe is from a favorite Bed and Breakfast in New York.*

Delaware's distinctive border with Pennsylvania, shaped like a circle, was drawn at the time of the original land grants to William Penn. King Charles, concerned that the newly created Pennsylvania not infringe on the Duke of York's holding to the south, ruled the boundary be set 12 miles from New Castle, resulting in a circular line between the two provinces.

It wasn't until 1751 that Delaware's southern border was formally surveyed. Fourteen years later, two famous Englishmen, Charles Mason and Jeremiah Dixon, drew the western boundary and then went on to mark the Pennsylvania-Maryland border, known ever since as the Mason-Dixon line.

Rum Raisin French Toast

Serves 4

¾ cup rum raisin ice cream, melted
3 eggs, beaten
⅓ cup ground walnuts
1 tablespoon dark rum
¼ teaspoon cinnamon
8 slices raisin bread
4 tablespoons butter, divided
Maple syrup, warmed, for topping
Additional ice cream, for topping (optional)

Combine the melted ice cream, eggs, walnuts, rum, and cinnamon in a shallow pan. Dip the bread slices in the ice cream mixture and let soak thoroughly, about a minute per side.

Melt 2 tablespoons of the butter in heavy skillet over medium heat. Place 4 soaked bread slices in the skillet and cook until browned, about 2 minutes per side. Repeat with the remaining butter and bread. Place 2 slices on each plate and serve immediately with warm maple syrup or a small scoop of ice cream.

♪ *The better the ice cream, the better the dish. Good for brunches.*

Southern Tomato Pie

Serves 6 to 8

2 refrigerated pie crusts, to fit a 9-inch pan
4 medium tomatoes, diced
1 medium onion, diced
1 cup mayonnaise
½ teaspoon dried basil
1½ cups Cheddar cheese
Salt and freshly ground black pepper to taste

Bake one of the pie crusts according to package directions and remove from the oven. Adjust the oven to 350°F. Combine the tomatoes, onions, mayonnaise, basil, cheese, salt, and pepper in a medium bowl, stirring until well blended. Pour into the baked crust and top with the uncooked top crust. Cook for 45 minutes, remove from the oven, and let stand a few minutes before slicing. Serve warm.

Macadamia Nut French Toast

Serves 8 to 10

4 eggs
⅔ cup orange juice
⅓ cup milk
¼ cup sugar
¼ teaspoon ground nutmeg
½ teaspoon pure vanilla extract
1 loaf Italian bread, cut in 1-inch-thick slices
⅔ cup butter, melted, plus additional for topping
½ cup macadamia nuts, diced
Maple syrup, for topping

Whisk together the eggs, orange juice, milk, sugar, nutmeg, and vanilla in a medium bowl until well combined. Place the bread slices in a single layer in a tight-fitting baking dish. Pour the milk mixture over the bread. Cover and refrigerate overnight, turning once. Preheat the oven to 400°F. Pour the melted butter in a jelly-roll pan, spreading evenly. Arrange the soaked bread slices in a single layer in the pan. Sprinkle with the macadamia nuts. Bake 20 to 25 minutes, or until golden brown. Serve hot with butter and warm maple syrup.

Some people give time, some money, some their skills and connections, some literally give their life's blood... but everyone has something to give.

~ Barbara Bush

Two-Cheese Tomato Quiche

Serves 4

1 unbaked pie shell
3 thick slices provolone cheese
½ cup chopped stuffed olives
½ cup chopped scallions
1 tablespoon butter
6 slices tomato
2 eggs
1 cup cream
2 cups grated sharp Cheddar cheese

Preheat the oven to 450°F. Bake the pie shell for 8 minutes. Remove from the oven and let cool. Reduce the oven to 350°F. Lay the provolone in the shell. Scatter the chopped olives and scallions and over the cheese. Heat a large skillet on medium-high and melt the butter. Sauté the tomato slices until golden brown. Layer the cooked tomatoes in the pie shell. Whisk together the eggs and cream. Stir in the Cheddar. Pour into pie shell and bake for 45 minutes until golden. Let stand 10 minutes before slicing to set.

Mushroom Pizza

Serves 4

1 (12 inch) prebaked pizza crust
3 tablespoons olive oil, divided
4 to 5 cloves garlic, minced
3 shallots thinly sliced
1 pound assorted mushrooms, sliced or chopped
⅓ cup dry red wine (optional)
1 ounce Gorgonzola cheese, crumbled
8 ounces well-chilled fontina cheese, grated or thinly sliced
Salt and freshly ground black pepper to taste

Put a pizza stone or pan in the oven and heat to 425°F. While the stone is heating, brush some olive oil evenly over the pizza crust and bake 5 to 7 minutes, or until the oil bubbles. While the shell bakes, begin cooking the toppings. Heat a large skillet on high and add the remaining oil. Quickly sauté the garlic and shallots for 30 seconds, being careful to not let the mixture burn. Add the mushrooms and sauté quickly until most of the mushroom juices have evaporated, about 3 to 5 minutes, then add the wine. Continue to sauté until the wine completely evaporates and the mushrooms have turned a darker shade. Remove the mushroom mixture from the heat.

Remove the crust from the oven and allow to cool slightly. Spread the Gorgonzola cheese evenly over the warm crust so that it melts slightly. (Dip your fingers in olive oil to spread the Gorgonzola more easily.) Spread the mushroom mixture evenly over the crust. Add the fontina cheese, as evenly as possible, and season with salt and pepper. Place on the hot stone and bake another 12 to 15 minutes, or until the cheese is lightly browned and bubbly. Let cool slightly and cut into small rectangles. Serve warm or at room temperature.

Use a meat baster to drop crêpe or pancake batter onto a hot griddle, and you'll get perfectly shaped pancakes every time.

~

Ebright Road in New Castle County is the highest elevation in the state, at 442 feet above sea level.

Spinach Quiche

Serves 4

1 (10 ounce) package frozen chopped spinach
3 eggs
2 tablespoons flour
¾ cups heavy cream
Salt to taste
¼ teaspoon freshly ground black pepper
8 ounces Cheddar cheese, shredded
4 slices bacon, cooked and crumbled
1 (9-inch) pastry shell, unbaked

Preheat the oven to 375°F. Cook the spinach, drain well, and squeeze dry. Combine the eggs, flour, cream, salt, and pepper. Stir in the spinach and cheese. Place the crumbled bacon in the bottom of the unbaked pie shell. Pour the spinach mixture over the bacon. Bake for 45 minutes, or until golden brown and bubbly. Let rest for 10 minutes before slicing.

Sausage and Cheese Breakfast Casserole

Good

Serves 12

8 to 10 slices white bread, cut into cubes
1 pound hot pork sausage, crumbled and cooked
2 cups grated sharp Cheddar cheese
12 large eggs
2 cups milk
3 teaspoons dry mustard
1 teaspoon salt
Freshly ground black pepper to taste

Preheat the oven to 350°F. Grease a 9 x 13-inch glass baking dish. Place the bread in the baking dish. Top with the cooked sausage and the cheese. Beat the eggs together with the milk, dry mustard, and salt in a large bowl. Season with pepper. Pour over the sausage mixture. Cover and refrigerate at least 30 minutes, and up to 12 hours. Bake the casserole until the center is set, about 50 minutes for a puffy golden brown. Cut into squares to serve.

♪ *Good for morning company.*

Delaware is known and loved throughout the region as "The Home of Tax Free Shopping!"

~

Soak bacon in cold water for a few minutes before placing it in the skillet; this will lessen its tendency to shrink and curl.

*The Playhouse Theatre
in Wilmington, built in 1913,
is the longest continuously
operating legitimate theater
in the nation.*

Asparagus Egg Bake
with Mornay Sauce

Serves 8

Eggs

2 tablespoons butter
¼ cup chopped onion
1 cup cubed cooked ham
8 eggs, beaten

Sauce

2 tablespoons butter
2 tablespoons all-purpose flour
1¼ cups milk
1 teaspoon chicken-flavor instant bouillon
2 ounces (½ cup) shredded Swiss cheese
¼ cup freshly grated Parmesan cheese

Topping

1 (15 ounce) can extra-long tender asparagus spears, drained
2 tablespoons unseasoned dry bread crumbs
1 teaspoon butter, melted

Preheat the oven to 350°F. Grease a 12 x 8-inch (2-quart) baking dish. For the eggs, melt the butter in a large skillet over medium-high heat. Sauté the onion until crisp-tender. Add the ham and eggs; cook until the eggs are just set, stirring occasionally.

To prepare the sauce, melt the butter in a medium saucepan over medium heat. Stir in the flour and bouillon; cook until smooth and bubbly. Gradually add the milk; cook until mixture boils and thickens, stirring constantly. Add the Swiss and Parmesan cheeses, and stir until smooth. Carefully fold the sauce into the scrambled eggs. Pour into the baking dish.

(The dish can be made ahead up to this point. Cover and refrigerate up to 3 hours before baking. Uncover and bake as directed.)

Bake for 20 to 25 minutes, or until the eggs are warmed through. Remove from oven. For the topping, arrange the asparagus spears over the baked eggs. Combine the bread crumbs with the melted butter and sprinkle over the top. Return to the oven and bake an additional 5 minutes.

Huevos Rancheros (Mexican Eggs)

Serves 4

1 to 2 tablespoons butter
1 medium onion, sliced
½ green bell pepper, sliced
3 cloves garlic, minced
2 stalks celery, diced
1 tablespoon chili powder
1 (4 ounce) can diced green chiles
1 (14 ounce) can tomatoes
4 eggs
Corn tortillas, warmed

Heat a large sauté pan on medium-high and melt the butter. Sauté the onion, green pepper, garlic, celery, and chili powder until the onion and pepper are limp. Add the green chiles and canned tomatoes, and stir to incorporate. Simmer until thick, about 45 minutes.

While the sauce is almost done, poach or fry the eggs according to taste. To serve, place 2 warmed tortillas on each plate, pour some sauce over the tortillas, and top each with an egg.

♪ *This dish works especially well with Bedeviled Bacon.*

William Penn gave Delaware's two lower counties the names that remain today: St. Jones became Kent, and Deal was changed to Sussex.

~

Penn also directed that a new town, Dover, be laid out on the St. Jones River as the seat of Kent County. A county court was established in a private home, and later in a tavern.

Bedeviled Bacon

Serves 4

1 egg, beaten
½ teaspoon dry mustard
½ teaspoon cayenne pepper
½ teaspoon vinegar
4 slices bacon
½ cup cracker crumbs

Preheat the oven to 400°F. Combine the egg, mustard, cayenne, and vinegar. Dip the bacon in the egg mixture, and then in the cracker crumbs. Place the bacon slices on a rack in a baking pan. Bake about 20 minutes, or until crisp.

♪ *This bacons tastes great with Huevos Rancheros.*

The Wilmington Blue Rocks,
a Class-A Minor League
baseball team, play their
home games at Judy Johnson
field in Frawley Stadium, in
downtown Wilmington.
Daniel Frawley was Mayor
of Wilmington from 1985-1992.
William Julius "Judy" Johnson
(1900-89) played baseball in
the Negro Leagues from 1920-
1936. In 1975, he became the
first player from Delaware
inducted into the National
Baseball Hall of Fame.

Berried Cantaloupe and Honey Dressing

Serves 4

1 cup plain yogurt
2 tablespoons honey
2 teaspoons grated orange zest
2 small cantaloupes, halved and seeded
2 cups raspberries
Orange zest curls, for garnish

To prepare the dressing, combine the yogurt, honey, and orange zest; mix until well blended. Cover and refrigerate. Cover and chill the cantaloupe and raspberries. To serve, place the cantaloupe halves in individual bowls. Fill the centers with raspberries. Drizzle with the dressing and garnish with orange zest.

Granola

Serves 8 to 10

5½ cups total combination of oatmeal, wheat germ, bran, rye flakes, and sesame seeds
½ cup chopped nuts, such as walnuts, almonds, cashews, pecans, or a combination
½ cup sweetener, such as molasses, honey, brown sugar, or a combination
1 cup dried fruit, such as raisins, currants, apricots, or combination

Preheat the oven to 300°F. Combine all the ingredients except the dried fruits. Place on a cookie sheet and bake at least 60 minutes, stirring every 15 minutes. Remove from the oven and cool, stirring occasionally. When cool, add the dried fruit and store in an airtight container until ready to serve.

♪ *A nutritious cereal or snack. Be creative, try different nuts, dried fruits and sweeteners.*

Above: The Georgia Dining Room, Winterthur

Right: Winterthur

Tango
Soups & Salads

The Georgia Dining Room, Winterthur

The Georgia Dining Room at Winterthur opened in 1972, and fulfilled Henry Francis du Pont's wish to have period architecture from all of the original 13 colonies. The table is set in the manner of the 1930s, reflecting the period in which the room was built.

Photograph courtesy of Winterthur

Winterthur

Winterthur Museum is the world's premiere collection of American decorative arts from 1640-1860, showcased in period rooms and exhibition galleries in the original Henry Francis du Pont country estate. The annual Yuletide at Winterthur tour takes visitors back in time to American's holiday celebrations of the 18th and 19th centuries.

Photograph courtesy of Winterthur

Cream of Carrot Soup

Serves 6

6 carrots, sliced

1 onion, sliced

1 or 2 Turkish bay leaves

3 cups homemade or canned chicken stock

2 tablespoons flour

3 tablespoons butter

1 cup light cream

Salt to taste

Chopped fresh parsley leaves, for garnish

Combine the carrots, onion, bay leaves, and stock in a large saucepan, and bring to a boil. Reduce the heat, cover, and simmer 45 minutes. Discard the bay leaves, and purée the carrot-stock mixture in a blender. Heat a large saucepan on medium and melt the butter. Remove from the heat and stir in the flour. Return to the heat and cook, stirring constantly, for a few minutes. Remove from the heat and stir in the carrot purée, whisking well. Return to the heat and bring to a boil, stirring constantly. Boil about 3 minutes. Reduce the heat and add the cream. Heat through, but do not let boil. Season with salt. Ladle into warm serving bowls and garnish with the parsley.

♪ *I have made this soup for years, and have received many compliments.*

Chester County was one of the three original counties in Pennsylvania, created by William Penn in 1682. Its name is derived from Cheshire (i.e. Chester-shire), England, from whence many of its early settlers came. Today, visitors are drawn not only to the beauty of Chester County's rolling countryside, but also to its well-preserved heritage, and the community's strong roots in horsemanship and the arts.

Cream of Mushroom Soup
Serves 6 to 8

*Freeze leftover wine
in ice cube trays and store
in ziplock plastic bags for use
in soups, stews, sauces
and casseroles.*

~

*The Chesapeake and
Delaware (C&D) Canal
was completed in 1829. Since
then, it has shaved nearly
300 miles from the voyages
of cargo ships bound for
Baltimore. A series of bridges
crosses the canal, connecting
Delaware's industrial
north with its
agricultural
south.*

6 tablespoons butter, divided
1 pound fresh mushrooms, sliced
⅓ cup chopped celery
⅓ cup chopped onion
Several sprigs of fresh parsley
2 carrots, quartered
2 cups chicken stock
2 tablespoons flour
2 cups light cream
2 tablespoons white wine or dry sherry
1 teaspoon salt
Dash of paprika
Dash of nutmeg
Fresh chives (optional)

Heat a large saucepan on medium-high and melt 4 tablespoons of
the butter. Sauté the mushrooms, celery, and onion until the onions
are limp and the mushrooms are partially cooked, about 5 minutes.
Add a few sprigs of parsley, the carrots, and stock. Simmer,
uncovered, for 20 minutes. Remove and discard the parsley and
carrots. Remove half of the mushrooms and place in blender. Purée
until smooth. Return the puréed mushrooms to the broth mixture.
Heat a large saucepan on medium and melt the remaining 2
tablespoons of butter. Whisk in the flour. Slowly pour in the cream,
whisking constantly until thoroughly incorporated and thickened.
Slowly stir in the broth mixture and wine. Season with the salt,
paprika, and nutmeg. Warm through, but do not boil. Serve in
warm soup bowls and garnish with fresh chives or a sprig of
parsley.

Pumpkin Mushroom Soup

Serves 6 to 8

¼ pound butter

1 onion, finely chopped

2 quarts mushrooms, sliced

¼ cup flour

⅛ cup chicken broth

1 (28 ounce) can pumpkin

1 teaspoon curry

½ teaspoon nutmeg

3½ ounces honey

1 pint heavy cream

Melt the butter in a large skillet over medium heat. Sauté the onion until soft. Add the mushrooms and cook over low heat until all the water from mushrooms has cooked out, about 10 minutes. Stir in the flour and let cook for 1 minute. Gradually add the chicken broth, stirring thoroughly to incorporate the flour. Stir in the pumpkin, curry, nutmeg, and honey. Simmer 10 to 15 minutes to let the flavors meld. Add the cream and warm through, but do not boil. Serve in warm soup bowls.

For a creative presentation, serve hot soups in individual hollowed-out rounds of sourdough or pumpernickel bread. Creamy soups look best in dark breads, while darker soups such as tomato or lentil stand out in lighter varieties of bread.

Tango

Longwood Gardens

In 1700, George Pierce acquired 402 acres from William Penn. Pierce's descendants farmed the land and in 1798, began planting an arboretum that by 1850 was one of the finest in the nation. The farm was purchased in 1906 by Pierre S. du Pont, who sought to preserve the trees. From 1907 until 1954, he personally designed most of Longwood Gardens as it is enjoyed today. Longwood now encompasses 1,050 acres of gardens, woodlands and meadows.

Potato Soup
Serves 10 to 12

6 medium potatoes (about 2 pounds), peeled and chopped
1 medium carrot, finely chopped
3 (14½ ounce) cans chicken broth
4 slices bacon
2 tablespoons butter or margarine
3 stalks celery, chopped
1 large onion
2½ cups light cream
Salt and freshly ground black pepper to taste
Shredded cheese, for garnish
Sliced green onions, for garnish

Combine the potatoes, carrot, and chicken broth in a 4-quart Dutch oven. Bring to a simmer and cook for 15 to 20 minutes, or until the potatoes and carrots are tender. Mash slightly in the saucepan. Cook the bacon in a large skillet until crisp. Drain the bacon on paper towels, reserving the drippings in the skillet. Crumble the bacon and set aside. Add the butter to the drippings in the skillet and cook the celery and onion until tender. Add the celery and onion to the potato mixture in the Dutch oven. Stir in the cream and season with salt and pepper. Cook, stirring frequently, until heated through. Serve in warm bowls and garnish with the crumbled bacon, shredded cheese, and green onion.

Delmarva Chicken Corn Chowder

Serves 6 to 8

4 strips bacon, diced

½ cup diced celery

½ cup diced carrots

½ cup diced onion

3 tablespoons flour

1 quart chicken stock, heated

2 cups potatoes, diced into ¼-inch cubes

2 cups diced, cooked chicken

2 cups puréed or cream style corn

1 cup fresh or frozen corn kernels

½ teaspoon poultry seasoning

1 cup heavy cream, room temperature

Salt and freshly ground black pepper to taste

Sauté the bacon in a large stock pot until crisp. Pour off the grease and add the celery, carrot, and onion, stirring frequently. Cook until tender. Stir in the flour and cook for 2 to 3 minutes. Pour the stock slowly into the vegetable mixture, whisking to incorporate the flour and scraping the browned bits from the bottom of the pan for flavor. Add the potatoes, chicken, corn, and poultry seasoning. Cook until the potatoes are tender. Add the cream and simmer for 3 to 4 minutes. Season with salt and pepper, and serve immediately in warm bowls.

Want to learn about the first Dutch settlement in 1631, the 1798 wreck of the HBM De Braak, the old Cape Henlopen lighthouse, or the bombardment of Lewes by the British in the War of 1812? Visit the Zwaanendael Museum in Lewes, Delaware. The museum building, highlighted by an ornamental gable with carved stonework, is adapted from the old town hall in Hoorn, Holland. It was built in 1931 to commemorate the 300th anniversary of the first European settlement in Delaware.

The only people with whom you should try to get even, are those who have helped you.

~ May Maloo

Jalapeño Chicken Corn Chowder

Serves 4 to 6

1½ cups chicken broth
3 cups canned or frozen whole kernel corn, divided
1 cup milk or light cream
1 to 2 fresh jalapeño peppers, seeded and finely chopped
¾ cup chopped, cooked chicken
¼ (7½ ounce) jar roasted red sweet peppers

Combine the chicken broth with half of the corn in a blender. Process until smooth. Combine the puréed mixture with the remaining ¾ cup corn in a medium saucepan over medium heat. Stir in the milk, jalapeño peppers, cooked chicken, and red peppers. Heat through and ladle into warm bowls.

♪ *This is great served with quesadillas or nachos.*

Easy Beef Soup

Serves 6

1½ pounds lean ground beef
1 cup chopped onion
1 clove garlic, finely chopped
1 (28 ounce) can tomatoes, with juice
6 cups water
6 beef bouillon cubes
¼ teaspoon freshly ground black pepper
½ cup uncooked orzo
1½ cups frozen peas, carrots, and corn vegetable blend

Cook the beef, onion, and garlic in large saucepan over medium-high heat until the beef is browned, stirring frequently to separate meat. Drain the grease.

Purée the tomatoes with their juice in a blender or food processor. Add the puréed tomatoes, water, bouillon cubes, and pepper to the ground beef. Bring to a boil. Reduce the heat to low and simmer, uncovered, for 20 minutes. Add the orzo and the frozen vegetables. Simmer 15 minutes more, or until the pasta is al dente and the vegetables are cooked through. Serve in warm bowls with hot French bread.

Brandied Crabmeat Bisque

Serves 6 to 8

5 tablespoons butter, divided
3 medium carrots, quartered
1 medium onion, chopped
¼ cup all-purpose flour
3 (8 ounce) bottles clam juice
2 tablespoons tomato paste
3 tablespoons brandy
1 cup heavy cream
1 (6 ounce) package crabmeat
Salt and freshly ground black pepper to taste
Sliced tomato, for garnish
Sliced carrot, for garnish

Heat a large skillet on medium-high and melt 2 tablespoons of the butter. Sauté the carrots and onion until the onion is translucent. Melt the remaining 3 tablespoons of butter in a 1-quart casserole dish. Whisk in the flour and cook 1 minute, or until bubbly. Whisk in 1 bottle of clam juice and cook 2 minutes until smooth. Add the sautéed carrots and onion, and whisk in the remaining clam juice, tomato paste, and brandy. Cover and cook 6 minutes until just simmering. Purée in a blender or with a handheld mixer. Strain the soup into a large bowl, pressing the solids with a wooden spoon to extract any liquid and flavor. Stir in the heavy cream and crabmeat. Season with salt and pepper. Cool to room temperature, and then cover and refrigerate at least 4 hours. Serve in chilled soup bowls and garnish with the tomato and carrot.

♪ *This versatile soup is delicious hot or cold.*

A mile west of the long-gone Fort Christina, a community called Willingtown rose on the riverbank and soon became a bustling center of trade with inland farms. In 1739, Willingtown received a royal charter of incorporation and a new name: Wilmington.

The Delaware Agricultural Museum and Village in Dover includes historic early American structures that were built in other Delaware towns, and moved to their present location. Visitors are transported back to the 1890s, as they visit a farmhouse and barn, a blacksmith shop, one-room school, country store, train station and grist/saw mill. There is also a 1700s Swedish log cabin, to give visitors a glimpse of what life was like for Delaware's earliest settlers.

French Onion Soup

Serves 6 to 8

3 tablespoons butter
4 to 5 large, sweet Vidalia or Spanish onions, thinly sliced or minced
3 cloves garlic, minced
2 tablespoons flour
3 (10½ ounce) cans condensed beef broth
3 cups water
1 bay leaf
Salt and freshly ground black pepper to taste
1 loaf French bread, sliced and toasted
8 slices Swiss or Provolone cheese

Heat a heavy skillet on medium and add the butter. Sauté the onions and garlic, stirring continuously until the onions are light brown. Sprinkle the onion-garlic mixture with the flour. Cook 1 minute, stirring continuously to cook out any flour taste. Transfer the onion mixture to a stock pot. Add the beef broth, water, and bay leaf. Bring to a boil, reduce heat, and simmer for 30 to 40 minutes. Discard the bay leaf. Season with salt and pepper to taste. Preheat the broiler. Pour into ovenproof individual crock dishes. Place a slice of toasted bread on top of the soup. Cover with a slice of cheese and place under the broiler for a few minutes until the cheese melts.

Italian Garden Soup

Serves 6 to 8

2 tablespoons olive oil, divided

3 onions

2 large cloves garlic, chopped

8 cups canned chicken broth

2 (15 ounce) cans white kidney beans, drained

4 carrots, chopped

4 celery stalks, chopped

1 green bell pepper, chopped

½ cup chopped fresh parsley leaves

1 teaspoon dried rosemary

1 bay leaf

1 pound mild Italian sausage

1 cup uncooked small pasta shells

12 stalks asparagus, trimmed and cut into 1-inch pieces

2 cups washed and shredded spinach leaves

¼ cup homemade or store-bought pesto sauce (optional)

Salt and freshly ground black pepper to taste

Freshly grated Parmesan cheese, for garnish (optional)

Heat a Dutch oven on medium-high and add 1 tablespoon of the olive oil. Sauté the onions and garlic until the onions are soft, about 10 minutes. Stir in the chicken broth, kidney beans, carrots, celery, green pepper, parsley, rosemary, and bay leaf. Bring the soup to a simmer and cook for 5 minutes. (The soup can be prepared up to 1 day ahead at this point. Cover and refrigerate until ready to complete.)

Heat the remaining tablespoon of olive oil in a heavy, medium skillet over medium-low heat. Add the sausage and cook about 20 minutes, or until cooked through. Drain the sausage on paper towels and then transfer to a cutting board. Cut the sausage into ½-inch-thick rounds. Add the sausage, pasta, asparagus pieces, and spinach to the soup and bring to a simmer. Cook for about 10 minutes, or until the pasta is al dente. Stir in the pesto, if desired, and season with salt and pepper. Sprinkle with Parmesan cheese, if desired.

Soups should not be salted until just before serving, since the saltiness intensifies as the stock is reduced.

~

If you accidentally over-salt a soup, sauce or stew while it's still cooking, drop in a peeled potato; it will absorb the excess salt.

Zesty Beef Soup
Serves 6 to 8

1 pound beef, such as round steak or stew meat
1 cup chopped onion
2 cloves garlic
1 teaspoon salt
1 teaspoon dried oregano leaves
1 teaspoon freshly ground black pepper
½ teaspoon dried sage
⅛ to ¼ teaspoon cayenne pepper
1 (48 ounce) can tomato juice
1 cup chopped celery
1 cup chopped potato
1 cup chopped carrots
1 cup chopped cabbage
4 beef bouillon cubes
6 cups water
⅓ cup uncooked wild rice

Brown the beef and sauté the onion and garlic in a large pan over medium-high heat. Combine the salt, oregano, pepper, sage, cayenne, tomato juice, celery, potato, carrots, cabbage, bouillon cubes, water, and rice in a large pot. Stir in the beef mixture. Bring to a boil, reduce the heat, and simmer for about an hour, or until the rice is cooked and the flavors have melded. Skim off any fat from the surface and serve in warm bowls.

♪ *Freezes well so you can make a double batch.*
This is a favorite with children.

What are those towers at the beach? After the Europeans resettled the Delaware coast following the Indians' destruction of the Dutch Colony, (Zwaanendael, in what is now Lewes), they had to be on guard for attacks from pirates. From the upper levels of these towers, observers scanned the Atlantic for enemy vessels. After Pearl Harbor, the towers were used once again, as it was believed the Delaware coast was in danger of attack by German submarines. This bombardment of coastal towns never occurred, and today, there are few reminders of those difficult days during World War II, except for the concrete towers that still stand like sentinels along the coast.

Beef Stew with Molasses and Raisins

Serves 6 to 8

3 pounds stew beef, trimmed and cubed

3 tablespoons flour

2 tablespoons oil

1 (28 ounce) can plum tomatoes

3 cups sliced onion

1 teaspoon celery salt

⅓ cup cider vinegar

½ cup sulfured molasses

1 cup water

1 cup baby carrots, or more to taste

½ cup raisins

½ teaspoon ground ginger

Toss the beef in the flour and shake off any excess. Set a Dutch oven over medium heat and add the oil. Sauté the beef in batches until browned. Add the tomatoes and onion; sauté for 2 minutes, scraping up any browned bits from bottom. Add the celery salt, vinegar, molasses, and water, stirring to blend. Cover and simmer for approximately 1½ hours, or until the beef is just tender. Add the carrots, raisins, and ginger. Cook 20 to 30 minutes more, or until the carrots are tender. Serve with broad egg noodles or bread.

♪ *The better the beef, the better the outcome-and it's even tastier on day two.*

Barley that's been "pearled" has had the tough outer hull of the grain removed. Pearl barley, medium barley, fine barley or plain barley are interchangeable, although cooking times may vary slightly. Quick-cooking barley becomes mushy, like oatmeal, when cooked, and should only be used if that texture is preferred.

Sausage and Tortellini Soup

Serves 6 to 8

1 pound sweet Italian sausage, casings removed
1 cup chopped onion
2 large cloves garlic, minced
5 cups beef stock
2 cups chopped tomatoes
1 (8 ounce) can tomato sauce
1 small zucchini, quartered and sliced
1 carrot, sliced
1 medium-size green bell pepper, chopped
½ cup red wine
2 tablespoons dried basil
2 tablespoons dried oregano
8 to 10 ounces store-bought cheese tortellini
Freshly grated Parmesan cheese

Sauté the sausage in a large skillet over medium heat for 10 minutes, stirring frequently to break up the meat. Add the onion and garlic, and continue cooking for 5 minutes. Stir in the beef stock, tomatoes, tomato sauce, and let cook 1 to 2 minutes. Add the zucchini, carrot, green pepper, red wine, basil, and oregano. Reduce the heat to low, cover, and cook about 40 minutes, or until the vegetables are just tender. Add the tortellini and cook about 8 more minutes, or until the pasta is al dente. Serve in warm, shallow soup bowls and garnish with Parmesan.

"It rained torrentially on the night of July 1, 1776…" That's how the story always begins. Caesar Rodney, one of Delaware's three delegates to the Continental Congress, had been summoned at his farm outside Dover; he was needed immediately at the State House ~ now Independence Hall ~ in Philadelphia. Hanging in the balance was Delaware's vote for independence from the British Crown. One of Delaware's delegates, Thomas McKean, favored separation, but George Read, a prominent member of Delaware's Colonial Assembly, was against it. If Rodney could arrive by the following day,

Lobster Stew

Serves 6

2 tablespoons butter
2 pounds fresh or frozen lobster meat
1 quart milk
½ cup heavy cream
Salt and freshly ground black pepper to taste

Heat a large saucepan on medium-high and melt the butter. Sauté the lobster until just cooked. Add the milk and bring to a boil. Add the cream, season with salt and pepper, and serve piping hot.

♪ *Serve with crusty French bread.*

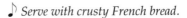

Southwestern Stew

Serves 8

2 tablespoons cooking oil

2 pounds beef stew meat, cut into 1-inch cubes

2 cups water

1¼ cups chopped onion

1 cup salsa

2 cloves garlic, minced

1 tablespoon dried parsley flakes

2 teaspoons beef bouillon granules

1 teaspoon ground cumin

½ teaspoon salt

3 medium carrots, cut into 1-inch pieces

1 (14½ ounce) can diced tomatoes, with juice

1½ cups frozen cut green beans

1½ cups frozen corn

1 (4 ounce) can chopped green chiles

Salt and freshly ground black pepper to taste

Hot pepper sauce (optional)

Heat a 4-quart Dutch oven on medium and add the oil. Brown the meat on all sides; drain. Add the water, onion, salsa, garlic, parsley, bouillon, salt, and cumin to the Dutch oven and bring to a boil. Reduce the heat, cover, and simmer for 1 hour. Add the carrots and return to a boil. Reduce the heat and simmer for 20 more minutes. Stir in the tomatoes, beans, corn, and chiles, and return to a boil. Reduce the heat, cover, and simmer for 15 to 20 minutes, or until the beef and vegetables are tender. Season with salt, pepper, and hot pepper sauce, if desired. Serve in warm soup bowls or over a bed of hot rice.

his vote would help decide the fate of Delaware ~ and the fledgling nation. Without stopping for sleep, Rodney rode 80 miles through the night, in sheets of rain and over primitive dirt roads that had turned to mud. When he finally arrived at the State House on the afternoon of July 2, he burst into the assembly chamber, tired and dusty, accompanied by an anxious McKean. After much debate among the delegates, Rodney declared his vote: He, and the Delaware delegation, favored independence!

Tuscan Lamb and Black Olive Stew

Serves 4 to 6

¼ **cup olive oil**
2 **cloves garlic, crushed**
2 **sprigs fresh rosemary**
1 **cup dry white wine**
2 **pounds lamb or veal, cut into 1-inch cubes**
1 **(14 ounce) can diced tomatoes**
1 **tablespoon grated lemon zest**
1 **cup canned black olives, rinsed well**
Salt and freshly ground black pepper to taste

Nonstick skillets are wonderful, but should not be used for deglazing (stirring wine or stock in a sauté pan after the food is removed). Only a hot skillet that allows for sticking, will sear meat with a tasty crust during sautéing, letting you capture those tidbits afterward to add flavor to your sauce.

Heat a large sauté pan on medium and add the oil. Sauté the garlic and rosemary until the garlic is golden. Increase the heat to medium-high and add the lamb to brown. Deglaze the pan with the wine, scraping up the browned bits for added flavor. When the liquid is almost completely reduced, add the tomatoes and the lemon zest. Reduce the heat to low, cover, and cook for 15 minutes. Add the olives-chop or slice them, if desired-and continue to cook, covered, for an hour or more, until the meat is tender. Add warm water or stock if the stew becomes too dry. Serve over polenta or couscous in shallow bowls.

Chili For A Crowd

Serves 15 to 20

¼ cup extra virgin olive oil

1 pound yellow onions, coarsely chopped

1 pound sweet Italian sausage, casings removed

4 pounds extra lean ground beef

1 tablespoon freshly ground black pepper, plus more to taste

1 (12 ounce) can tomato paste

2 tablespoons minced garlic

3 ounces ground cumin

4 ounces plain chile powder

¼ cup Dijon mustard

2 tablespoons dried basil

2 tablespoons dried oregano

3 (28 ounce) cans Italian plum tomatoes, drained and coarsely chopped

½ cup dry red wine

Juice of 1 lemon

½ cup chopped fresh dill leaves

½ cup chopped fresh Italian parsley leaves

2 (16 ounce) cans dark red kidney beans, drained

2 (5½ ounce) cans pitted black olives, drained

Salt to taste

Sour cream, for garnish

Grated Cheddar cheese, for garnish

Chopped green onions, for garnish

Heat the olive oil in a large Dutch oven on medium. Add the onions, reduce the heat to low, and cook until tender and translucent, about 10 minutes.

Crumble the sausage meat and ground beef into the pot and increase the heat to medium-high. Cook until well browned, stirring often to break up the meat. Reduce the heat to low and stir in the black pepper, tomato paste, garlic, cumin, chile powder, mustard, basil, and oregano. Add the tomatoes, wine, lemon juice, dill, parsley and kidney beans. Stir well and simmer, uncovered, for another 15 minutes. Season with salt and pepper to taste. Add the olives, simmer for another 5 minutes to heat through. For a complete meal, serve over rice and top with sour cream, grated Cheddar cheese, and chopped onions.

Chipotle chiles are smoked, dried jalapeños, and are most commonly canned in adobo sauce (a mixture of ground chiles, herbs and vinegar). Chipotle chiles can also be bought dried. Although these can be rehydrated, it is better to grind them into a powder, so that you can add small amounts to a recipe gradually. Slice each chili in half lengthwise, and remove the seeds. Arrange them on a baking sheet and roast at 300°F about 5 minutes, until chiles are completely dried. Cool, then transfer to a food processor or spice grinder and process until you have a fine powder. Store in refrigerator or freezer in an airtight container for up to one year.

Cayenne peppers and chiles get their heat from the chemical capsaicin. Capsaicin is not water-soluble, but will dissolve in either fat or alcohol. Therefore, to cut the "fire" from eating a bowl of hot chili, drink a glass of cold milk or a chilled beer.

White Chicken Chili

Serves 8 to 10

1 pound dried small white navy beans
7 cups chicken broth, or more if needed
2 cloves garlic
2 medium onions, chopped and divided
1 tablespoon olive oil
2 (4 ounce) cans mild green chiles
2 teaspoons cumin
1½ teaspoons dried oregano
¼ teaspoon ground cloves
¼ teaspoon cayenne pepper
4 cups diced cooked chicken
3 cups grated Monterey Jack cheese
Sour cream or plain, non-fat yogurt, for topping
Salsa, for topping
Chopped green onions, for topping

Combine the beans, chicken broth, garlic, and half the onion in a large pot. Bring to a boil, reduce the heat, and simmer until the beans are soft, about 3 hours. Heat a medium sauté pan on medium and add the oil. Sauté the remaining onion, and then add the green chiles, cumin, oregano, cloves, and cayenne, mixing thoroughly. Add the onion mixture to the beans. Add the chicken, cover, and simmer for 1 hour. (Add more broth if needed.) To serve, ladle into warm bowls, sprinkle with some cheese, top with a dollop of sour cream and salsa, and garnish with green onion.

♪ *Tortilla chips or Mexican corn bread are great with this chili. If you're in a hurry, the roasted whole chickens available in the supermarket are a good alternative for the cooked chicken.*

Black Pepper-
Pineapple Vinaigrette

Serves 4 to 6

1 medium pineapple, peeled and diced
½ cup freshly squeezed lime juice
½ cup rice vinegar
2 tablespoons peanut oil
3 star anise
½ teaspoon black peppercorns

Combine all the ingredients in a food processor or blender, and process until quite smooth. Chill. Serve over mixed greens, fruit salad, or seafood.

In addition to flowers and fountains, Longwood Gardens features a 10,000-pipe organ in the Conservatory.

Creamy Honey
Mustard Vinaigrette

Serves 6 to 8

⅓ cup cider vinegar
⅓ cup Dijon mustard
⅓ cup honey
1 cup canola oil
Dash of salt

Whisk together the vinegar and mustard in a small mixing bowl. Slowly drizzle in the honey, whisking continuously to incorporate. Continue whisking and drizzle in the oil until emulsified. Season with salt. Store in a jar in the refrigerator for up to 2 weeks. Shake well before using.

♪ *Excellent on spinach salad!*

Raspberry Vinaigrette
Serves 4 to 6

½ tablespoon olive oil plus ¼ cup olive oil, divided
2 tablespoons raspberry vinegar
½ tablespoon Creole or Dijon mustard
¼ teaspoon salt
¼ teaspoon freshly ground black pepper

Whisk ½ tablespoon of the olive oil with the vinegar, mustard, salt, and pepper. Drizzle in the remaining ¼ cup of olive oil, whisking continuously to emulsify.

To peel peaches, bring a medium saucepan of water to a boil. Gently drop in one peach at a time, for 5 seconds, retrieving it by piercing with a fork. With a paring knife, slit the skin, which will slip off easily.

Peach Salad
Serves 9 to 12

3 to 4 (10½ ounce) cans peach halves, with juice
1 cup crushed cereal, preferably Total
¼ cup packed dark brown sugar
¼ teaspoon salt
1½ tablespoons flour
⅛ cup white corn syrup
¼ teaspoon freshly squeezed lemon juice
1½ tablespoons butter, melted
¼ cup chopped pecans

Preheat the oven to 350°F. Drain the peaches on paper towels and reserve the juice. Combine the cereal, brown sugar, salt, and flour in a medium bowl, stirring well. Add ⅛ cup of the reserved peach juice, the corn syrup, lemon juice, butter, and pecans. Fill the center of the peaches with the mixture and place in a large casserole dish. (The dish tastes best if refrigerated at this point for several hours. Bring to room temperature before baking.) Bake for 30 to 35 minutes and serve warm.

Black Beans and Corn with Salsa Dressing

Serves 6

1 (15 ounce) can black beans, rinsed and drained
1 cup cooked whole kernel corn
1 red bell pepper, seeded and cut into ½-inch pieces (about ¾ cup)
1 stalk celery with leaves, sliced (⅔ cup)
1 tablespoon snipped fresh cilantro or parsley leaves
¼ cup plain yogurt
¼ cup mayonnaise or salad dressing
¼ cup salsa
Lettuce leaves (optional)
½ medium avocado, peeled, pitted, and sliced (optional)

Combine the beans, corn, red pepper, celery, and cilantro in a large bowl. To make the dressing, combine the yogurt, mayonnaise, and salsa in small bowl. (The dressing can be made up to 1 week ahead of time and stored in an airtight container in the refrigerator.)

Add the dressing to the bean mixture and toss to coat. Cover and chill for 2 to 24 hours. If desired, serve in salad bowls lined with lettuce leaves and garnish with avocado slices.

The DuPont Company first produced nylon at its plant in Seaford, Delaware, earning the town the distinction of "Nylon Capital of the World."

~

The Governor Ross Mansion and Plantation is now owned by the Seaford Historical Society. Here, on a 20-acre, Civil War-era plantation, is a brick, Italian Villa-style mansion (c. 1859), a granary, carriage house, barns, corn crib, ham house, a restored honeymoon cottage, and Delaware's only documented log slave quarters.

Chicken Salad with Artichokes

Serves 8 to 10

4 chicken breasts, cooked and cubed
1 (14 ounce) can artichoke hearts, drained and chopped
¾ cup mayonnaise
¾ cup chopped celery
6 green onions, chopped
1 cup chopped pecans, toasted
¼ teaspoon salt
⅛ teaspoon pepper
⅛ teaspoon garlic powder
¼ teaspoon curry powder

Combine all the ingredients in a medium bowl. Cover and refrigerate until ready to use. Serve on bread or over lettuce leaves.

The British were not about to surrender the colonies without a fight. In late summer of 1777, Delaware took center stage in the battle for independence. Convinced that occupying Philadelphia was the key to winning the war, the British commander, Gen. William Howe, landed 15,000 men at the head of the Chesapeake Bay and began a march across Delaware toward the Continental capital. To oppose the Redcoats, Gen. George Washington stationed a large force along the Red Clay Creek, dispatching more than 700 infantrymen forward to the woods near Newark and Glasgow, with instructions "to give {the British} as much trouble as you possibly can." Tradition holds that Betsy Ross' 13-star flag, the Stars and

Black Bean and Rice Salad

Serves 6 to 8

½ cup olive oil
¼ cup apple cider vinegar
1 tablespoon Dijon mustard
1 teaspoon ground cumin
2 cloves garlic, minced
Salt and freshly ground black pepper to taste
2½ cups cooked long-grain white rice (about 1 cup raw), cooled
1 (15 ounce) can black beans, drained and rinsed
¾ cup chopped orange or red bell pepper
¾ cup chopped yellow bell pepper
¾ cup chopped green onion

Whisk the oil, vinegar mustard, cumin, and garlic in a large salad bowl. Season with salt and pepper. Add the rice, beans, bell peppers, and green onion. Toss well to mix. Cover and chill before serving.

♪ *This is a perfect summer salad.*

Fresh Fig, Gorgonzola, and Walnut Salad

Serves 6 to 8

1 pound arugula or mesclun mix, stemmed
12 fresh figs, halved lengthwise
2 cups Gorgonzola cheese, crumbled
1¾ cups walnuts, toasted and chopped
1 cup ruby port wine
1 tablespoon sugar
¼ cup balsamic vinegar
¾ cup extra virgin olive oil
Freshly ground black pepper

Rinse, drain, and dry the greens well. Place in mounds on 8 small or 4 large salad plates. Top with fig halves, crumbled cheese, and toasted walnuts. Reduce the port wine by half over medium-high heat in a small saucepan, being careful not to ignite the wine. Add the sugar and stir to dissolve. Remove from heat. Add the balsamic vinegar. Slowly whisk in the olive oil. While still warm, drizzle over each salad. Lightly season with pepper.

Roasted Corn, Black Bean, and Mango Salad

Serves 6 to 8

1 tablespoon vegetable oil

3 cloves garlic, minced

3 cups fresh corn kernels (6 ears)

2 cups diced ripe mango

1 cup chopped red onion

1 cup chopped red bell pepper

⅓ cup freshly squeezed lime juice

3 tablespoons chopped fresh cilantro leaves

½ teaspoon salt

½ teaspoon ground cumin

1 (4 ounce) can chopped green chiles

2 (15 ounce) cans black beans, drained and rinsed

8 cups field greens (optional)

Heat a large, nonstick skillet on medium-high and add the oil. Sauté the garlic for 30 seconds. Stir in the corn and cook for 8 minutes, or until browned, stirring occasionally. Place the corn mixture in a large bowl. Add the mango, red onion, red pepper, lime juice, cilantro, salt, cumin, green chiles, and black beans. Stir well. Serve over field greens, if desired.

Stripes, was first unfurled in this heated "Battle of Cooch's Bridge" on September 3, 1777. The "Battle of Brandywine," September 11, 1777, headed north through Newark, DE, to Kennett Square and Chadds Ford, PA, and then on to Wilmington and finally Philadelphia.

The flowers of kitchen herbs and other edible blooms make delicate, colorful decorations for a variety of foods. Bright nasturtium flowers, calendula petals, or soft chive blossoms are good on green salads, meat or fish; white basil flowers add a fresh touch to sliced tomatoes; and tiny sprigs of rosemary, with their mauve flowers, are beautiful on lemon desserts.

Citrus Couscous Salad

Serves 8

1 cup chicken or vegetable broth
1 cup couscous
½ cup orange juice
6 tablespoons olive oil
3 tablespoons white vinegar
3 tablespoons freshly squeezed lemon juice
¼ cup chopped scallions
¼ cup chopped fresh cilantro leaves
2 teaspoons soy sauce
2 teaspoons grated orange zest
2 teaspoons peeled and chopped fresh ginger
Salt and freshly ground black pepper to taste
2 oranges, peeled and cut into segments, or 1 small can mandarin oranges
¼ cup pine nuts, toasted (optional)

Bring the chicken broth to a boil in a small saucepan. Place the couscous in a medium bowl and pour in the boiling broth and orange juice. Stir, cover, and set aside, stirring occasionally until all the broth is absorbed, about 5 to 10 minutes. Fluff with a fork.

Whisk together the oil, vinegar, lemon juice, scallions, cilantro, soy sauce, orange zest, ginger, salt, and pepper in small bowl. Add to the couscous, mixing well.

Serve immediately or chill for 30 minutes. Stir in the oranges and pine nuts just before serving.

Tomato Salad

Serves 4 to 6

3 or 4 tomatoes, coarsely chopped
1 (3.8 ounce) can sliced black olives
1 small red onion, thinly sliced
¼ to ½ cup chopped green bell pepper
8 ounces feta cheese, crumbled
Chopped scallions to taste
⅛ cup balsamic vinegar
⅛ cup olive oil
Dash of garlic powder
2 teaspoons dried basil, or more to taste
½ teaspoon dried oregano
Freshly ground black pepper to taste

Toss the tomatoes, olives, onion, green pepper, feta cheese, and scallions in a large serving bowl. Combine the vinegar, olive oil, pepper, garlic powder, basil, and oregano in a small bowl, mixing well. Season with pepper. Pour the oil mixture over the tomatoes and toss to coat. Cover and let marinate in the refrigerator for several hours before serving.

♪ *Best prepared with fresh summer tomatoes.*

Caesar Rodney made his mark on Delaware, and the nation, in July of 1776, as he rode through thunder and rain from his farm in Kent County to Philadelphia, to cast his deciding vote for Independence. He is depicted in a beautiful statue in the middle of Rodney Square in downtown Wilmington, and on the Delaware state quarter.

~

In the churchyard beside Christ Episcopal Church in Dover is a memorial to Caesar Rodney, but the exact location of his grave remains a mystery.

Here's an easy way to make your own croutons: Put 1 to 2 tablespoons of olive oil in the bottom of a Pyrex baking dish. Cube leftover French bread, removing most of the crusts, and toss to coat with oil. Sprinkle with Italian herbs and garlic and toss again. Microwave 2 minutes on high, then brown in oven at 425°F for 3 to 10 minutes. (Check often, tossing occasionally so all sides brown.) Croutons keep for several weeks in an airtight container.

Asparagus-Artichoke-Mushroom Salad

Serves 6 to 8

½ **pound fresh asparagus spears, trimmed**
1 **(6 ounce) jar marinated artichoke hearts, with juice**
½ **cup sliced mushrooms**
¼ **cup sliced spring onions**
1 **tablespoon vinegar**
1 **teaspoon sugar**
1 **teaspoon sesame seeds, toasted**
¼ **teaspoon salt**
Several dashes of Tabasco sauce
Shredded lettuce, such as iceberg or Bibb

Place the asparagus in a steamer basket set over boiling water. Cover tightly and steam until crisp-tender. Rinse in cold water to stop the cooking process, and then drain. Place in a rectangular glass dish. Drain the artichoke hearts, reserving the marinade, and slice any large hearts in half. Layer the artichokes on top of the asparagus. Add the mushrooms and spring onions. Combine the reserved marinade with the vinegar, sugar, sesame seeds, salt, and Tabasco in a small jar; shake to emulsify. Pour the dressing over the layered vegetables, cover, and refrigerate for several hours. Place the lettuce on a serving platter. Remove the vegetables from the marinade and arrange on top the lettuce.

Rocky Mountain Salad

Serves 6 to 8

⅓ cup chopped onion

3 tablespoons cider vinegar

2 teaspoons spicy brown mustard

1 teaspoon sugar

½ teaspoon salt

¼ teaspoon freshly ground black pepper

¾ cup olive oil

2 heads romaine lettuce, torn into bite-size pieces

1 (14 ounce) can water-packed artichoke hearts, drained and quartered

1 large avocado, peeled, seeded, and diced

½ pound bacon, crisply cooked and crumbled

4 ounces freshly grated Parmesan cheese

Combine the onion and vinegar in a food processor or blender until the onion is puréed. Add the mustard, sugar, salt, and pepper, and pulse to combine Gradually drizzle in the olive oil in a steady stream, processing continuously until emulsified. Combine the lettuce, artichoke hearts, avocado, bacon, and cheese in a large bowl. Add enough dressing to coat well. Toss thoroughly and serve immediately on chilled plates.

♪ *This is a great alternative to a Caesar.*

The best salads have a balance of textures, colors and tastes. Contrast crunchy ingredients with smooth dressings, vibrant colors with muted hues, and mellow flavors with spicy or bold tastes.

Italian Salad

Serves 6 to 8

Salad

5 cups washed and torn fresh spinach

3 cups red leaf lettuce

1 sweet yellow pepper, cut into strips

⅔ cup thinly sliced radishes

1 small red onion, sliced and separated into rings

Dressing

3 tablespoons red wine vinegar

6 teaspoons olive oil

¾ teaspoon garlic salt

¾ teaspoon dried oregano, crushed

2 tablespoons freshly grated Parmesan cheese

Combine the salad ingredients and toss to mix. To prepare the dressing, combine the vinegar, olive oil, garlic salt, and oregano in a small jar. Cover and shake well. Pour the dressing over the salad, add the Parmesan, and toss lightly to coat. Serve immediately on chilled salad plates.

Lettuce is like conversation: it must be fresh and crisp, and so sparkling that you scarcely notice the bitter in it.

~ Charles Dudley Warner

Splendid Raspberry Spinach

Serves 6 to 8

2 tablespoons raspberry vinegar

2 tablespoons raspberry jam

⅓ cup vegetable oil

8 cups spinach, washed thoroughly, stemmed, and torn into pieces

¾ cup coarsely chopped macadamia nuts, divided

1 cup fresh raspberries, divided

3 kiwis, peeled and sliced, divided

To prepare the dressing, combine the vinegar and jam in blender or small bowl. Add the oil in a thin stream, blending well. Combine the spinach with half of the nuts, half of the raspberries, and half of the kiwis on a platter or flat salad bowl. Toss with the dressing. Top with the remaining nuts, raspberries, and kiwis. Serve immediately on chilled salad plates.

Three-Way Strawberry-Spinach Salad

Serves 4 to 6

Salad

1 bunch fresh spinach or 1 head romaine or red leaf lettuce, washed thoroughly, dried, and torn into bite-size pieces
½ medium-size red onion, sliced
1 pint strawberries, hulled and quartered
¼ cup slivered almonds, lightly toasted

Dressing One

¼ cup sugar
1½ teaspoons minced green onion
¼ teaspoon paprika
¼ teaspoon Worcestershire sauce
1 tablespoon poppy seeds
¼ cup rice vinegar

Dressing Two

¼ cup sugar
¼ cup cider vinegar
1½ teaspoons minced onion
¼ teaspoon paprika
¼ teaspoon Worcestershire sauce
½ cup vegetable oil
1 tablespoon poppy seeds

Dressing Three

2 tablespoons balsamic vinegar
2 teaspoons red wine vinegar
⅓ cup vegetable oil
½ cup plain, non-fat yogurt
⅓ teaspoon salt
⅔ cup sugar
1 teaspoon poppy seeds
⅔ teaspoon dry mustard

The town of Delmar is known as "the little town too big for one state." It is divided in two by the Maryland/Delaware boundary, which also happens to be the Mason-Dixon Line. This is the only portion of the Mason-Dixon line that runs North-South.

Place the spinach in a large salad bowl. Add the onion, strawberries, and almonds. Prepare one of the dressings listed above: combine all the ingredients in a small jar and shake to emulsify. Before serving, pour the prepared dressing over the greens and toss to coat. Serve on chilled salad plates.

Pick the Right Pear

• *Bosc: This Belgian pear with brownish-gold skin is among the slimmest varieties, with a lovely curved shape. Its distinct flavor has been compared to vanilla, caramel and brown butter. This pear is best used for cooking because of its firm texture, which allows it to hold its shape and retain its juices.*

• *Anjou: Named for the historic region in northwestern France known for its pears, the Anjou is a large, rounded fruit that has green skin, often with a red "blush." Anjou pears are very juicy and have a mild, delicate flavor. Choose under-ripe fruit for cooking, to help these pears retain their shape. Otherwise, they are wonderful eaten fresh, when they are ripe enough to yield gently to the touch.*

Spinach Pear Salad

Serves 4 to 6

Salad

3 cups baby spinach, washed thoroughly and dried

3 medium-size ripe yellow pears, cored but not peeled, cut lengthwise into slices

2 tablespoons crumbled bleu cheese

¼ cup chopped walnuts, lightly toasted

Dressing

2 tablespoons balsamic vinegar

3 tablespoons olive oil

3 tablespoons orange juice

1 clove crushed garlic

Place the spinach, pears, and cheese in a medium salad bowl. Whisk together the dressing ingredients and pour over the salad. Toss the dressing with the salad. Sprinkle with the warm, toasted walnuts and serve immediately.

Marinated Bean Sprout Salad

Serves 4 to 6

1 bag bean sprouts

3 tablespoons chopped scallions

2 tablespoons sesame oil

2 tablespoons soy sauce

1 tablespoon vinegar

Blanch the bean sprouts in boiling water until crisp-tender. Rinse in cold water to stop the cooking process. Combine the scallions, sesame oil, soy sauce, and vinegar in a small bowl. Toss the marinade with the sprouts. Cover and marinate in the refrigerator for at least 1 hour before serving.

♪ *Great with steak.*

Island Turkey Salad

Serves 4 to 6

1½ cups chopped, cooked white turkey or chicken meat

¾ cup chopped celery

¼ cup chopped green onions

1 (6 ounce) can water chestnuts, drained and sliced

1 cup seedless grapes

1 (8 ounce) can pineapple chunks, well drained

1 cup mayonnaise

1 tablespoon freshly squeezed lemon juice

1¼ tablespoons soy sauce

1½ teaspoons curry powder

1 tablespoon chopped mango chutney

¼ cup slivered almonds, toasted

Combine the turkey or chicken, celery, green onions, water chestnuts, grapes, and pineapple chunks in a large bowl. Combine the mayonnaise, lemon juice, soy sauce, curry powder, and chutney in a small bowl. Add the mayonnaise mixture to the salad and toss to coat well. Cover and chill, preferably overnight. Serve in a papaya or pineapple half, or on a bed of lettuce. Garnish with the almonds.

• *Bartlett: Enoch Bartlett introduced this English pear to New England in the eighteenth century. Because of its sweetness and juiciness, it's the preferred pear for packaged products (like fruit cocktail and bottled fruit juice) and for eating fresh. It is also fine for baking, if slightly under-ripe. Green Bartletts will turn yellow when ripe; red Bartletts are also available, with a slightly stronger "pear" flavor.*

*Bury avocados in
a bowl of flour to ripen.*

~

*Another Delaware
patriot was John Dickinson,
dubbed the "Penman of
the Revolution" for his
writings on independence.
Just south of the Dover
Air Force Base is his
boyhood home, now aptly
called the John Dickinson
Plantation.*

Avocado Delight Salad

Serves 6 to 8

1 (15 ounce) can black beans
3 tablespoons vegetable oil
2 tablespoons cider vinegar
½ teaspoon sugar
½ teaspoon salt
2 teaspoons minced pickled jalapeño pepper
2 avocados, peeled, pitted, and chopped
1 tomato, chopped
¼ cup chopped fresh cilantro leaves

Bring the black beans to a simmer for 5 minutes in a small sauce-pan. Drain and rinse under cold water. Combine the oil, vinegar, sugar, and salt in a medium bowl and whisk thoroughly. Add the jalapeño, avocado, tomato, beans, and cilantro to the dressing. Toss gently, cover, and chill until ready to serve. Serve on large lettuce leaves or with tortilla chips.

Make Your Mayo Dance!!

When using regular or nonfat mayonnaise on sandwiches, or in tuna or chicken salad, give it a flavor boost by stirring ½ cup with any of the following:

~ **Basil Mayo:** ½ cup fresh basil leaves, chopped.

~ **Dried Tomato Mayo:** 6 dried tomatoes (packed in oil ~ drained and minced).

~ **Lemon Mayo:** 1 teaspoon grated lemon rind and 2 tablespoons fresh lemon juice.

~ **Mediterranean Mayo:** 2 tablespoons chopped fresh parsley, 2 tablespoons minced green onions, 1 tablespoon chopped capers and 1 teaspoon hot sauce.

~ **Onion Mayo:** Sauté ½ cup chopped onion in nonstick skillet coated with cooking spray. Add 3 tablespoons water, simmer 5 minutes and add to mayo.

~ **Roasted Red Pepper Mayo:** ¼ cup coarsely chopped roasted sweet red peppers.

Ginger Chicken Salad

Serves 4

3 tablespoons sesame seeds

½ teaspoon salt

½ teaspoon freshly ground black pepper

4 (4 to 6 ounce) boneless, skinless chicken breasts, trimmed of fat

1 tablespoon olive oil

4 tablespoons rice vinegar

4 tablespoons soy sauce

2 tablespoons honey

4 teaspoons peeled and grated fresh ginger

2 teaspoons dry mustard

2 teaspoons sesame oil

½ teaspoon crushed red pepper flakes

½ pound fresh baby greens or romaine lettuce

Combine the sesame seeds, salt, and pepper in a small bowl. Sprinkle both sides of the chicken breasts with the sesame mixture. Heat a large skillet on medium and add the olive oil. Sauté the chicken pieces until cooked through, and then remove from the pan.

Combine the rice vinegar, soy sauce, honey, ginger, mustard, sesame oil, and red pepper. Bring to a boil, and then remove from the heat.

Divide the lettuce among 4 salad plates and slice the chicken breast diagonally to create thin strips. Place the chicken on top of the salad and drizzle with the dressing.

There are several ways to store fresh ginger, depending on how long you plan to keep it. Unpeeled ginger should be wrapped in a paper towel, sealed in a plastic bag, and stored in the refrigerator's vegetable crisper, where it will stay fresh for two to three weeks. For long-term storage, peel the ginger and rinse it under cold water. Then place it in a glass jar, cover with sherry, and refrigerate; it will keep for up to one year.

Tango

The Brandywine
River Museum, founded in
1971 with 12 paintings, was
originally supposed to be open
only during the summer
months. Today there are over
2,836 objects in the permanent
collection, and the museum
is open every day except
Christmas. There are 9,787
objects in the N.C. Wyeth
House and Studio collection,
which is also owned by
the museum.

Mandarin Salad

Serves 4 to 6

Salad

½ cup sliced almonds
3 tablespoons sugar
½ head iceberg lettuce, torn
½ head romaine lettuce, torn
1 cup chopped celery
2 green onions, white and green parts chopped
1 (11 ounce) can Mandarin oranges, drained

Dressing

½ teaspoon salt
Freshly ground black pepper
¼ cup vegetable oil
1 tablespoon chopped fresh parsley leaves
2 tablespoons sugar
2 tablespoons vinegar
Dash of Tabasco sauce

Cook the almonds and sugar in a small saucepan over medium heat, stirring constantly until the almonds are coated and the sugar is dissolved. Watch carefully so they don't burn. Spread the almonds out on wax paper to cool, and then store in an airtight container.

To prepare the dressing, combine all the ingredients in a small jar and shake to emulsify. Chill. When ready to serve, combine the iceberg, romaine, celery, and onions. Add the almonds and oranges, and toss with the dressing. Divide among chilled salad plates to serve.

Sesame Noodle Salad

Serves 6 to 8

1 pound uncooked spaghetti or linguine

⅓ cup sesame oil

1 tablespoon olive oil

10 scallions, chopped

4 cloves garlic, chopped,

½ teaspoon peeled and minced fresh ginger

½ teaspoon crushed red pepper flakes

2 tablespoons rice vinegar

2 tablespoons honey

¼ cup reduced-salt soy sauce

½ cup chopped fresh cilantro leaves

¼ cup chopped fresh parsley leaves

1 cup chopped peanuts

1 cucumber, diced

Cook the pasta in a large pot of boiling, salted water until al dente. Combine the sesame oil with the olive oil in a small bowl. Drain the pasta and toss with half of the oil mixture. Heat a large skillet on medium-high and add the remaining oil. Sauté the scallions, garlic, ginger, and red pepper. Blend together the rice vinegar, honey, and soy sauce in a small bowl and stir into the sautéed mixture. Add the parsley, cilantro, and peanuts. Toss with the pasta and garnish with diced cucumber. Serve at room temperature.

*Brandywine Battlefield Park encompasses 50 acres of land in Chadds Ford, Pennsylvania.
The Park contains historic houses used as headquarters by General Washington and quarters for General Lafayette during the Battle of Brandywine, one of the largest battles of the American Revolutionary War.*

Szechuan Noodle Salad

Serves 6 to 8

Dressing

1 clove garlic, minced
2 teaspoons dried basil
¼ teaspoon freshly ground black pepper
⅓ cup red wine vinegar
⅓ cup soy sauce
⅓ cup dark sesame oil
1 tablespoon hot chile oil

Salad

1 pound rotini pasta
1 bunch scallions, chopped
3 large carrots, sliced
2 cups frozen peas, cooked according to package directions

To prepare the dressing, combine the garlic, basil, and pepper in small bowl. Whisk in the vinegar and soy sauce. Slowly drizzle in the sesame oil and hot chile oil, whisking continuously to emulsify.

Cook the pasta in a large pot of boiling, salted water until al dente. Drain and place in large bowl. Add the scallions, carrots, and cooked peas. Pour with the dressing and toss well. Serve at room temperature or chilled. (The salad can be prepared up to 1 day in advance.)

The Barns-Brinton House was William Barns' Tavern in the 1720s. The Chadds Ford Historical Society purchased this handsome brick building in 1969, and has authentically restored it and furnished it as a country tavern. The interior is well known for its fine woodwork and paneling. Fortunately, much of the original hardware remains, probably wrought by blacksmith Barns. Listed on the National Register of Historic Places, the Barns-Brinton House is part of the Brandywine Battlefield National Historic Landmark.

Chinese Chicken Salad

Serves 4

Dressing

2 teaspoons dry mustard
4 tablespoons sugar
6 tablespoons rice vinegar
2 teaspoons soy sauce
2 tablespoons sesame oil
½ cup vegetable oil

Salad

Romaine lettuce, torn into bite-size pieces
2 stalks celery, chopped
24 snow peas
6 scallions, chopped
4 chicken breasts
1 cup chopped cashews
Chinese noodles

Combine all the dressing ingredients in a jar and shake to emulsify. Combine all the salad ingredients in a bowl. Drizzle with the dressing and toss to coat thoroughly. Serve on chilled plates.

A Guide to Gourmet Greens

Perk up your salads with the addition of interesting textures, colors and tastes using the following greens:

~ *Frisée* ~ A curly endive that lightens a salad with its delicate, lacy texture and mild, nutty flavor;

~ *Mache* ~ A Mediterranean delicacy with tongue-shaped leaves, to toss with soft Bibb or Boston lettuce;

~ *Mizuna* ~ This Asian mustard green adds unique feathery texture to salads of baby mixed greens;

~ *Radicchio* ~ Wine-red Italian chicory with brilliant white ribs and a bittersweet flavor gives salads a colorful kick;

~ *Arugula* ~ An herb and salad green with fresh, young leaves that adds texture and a "toasted" flavor to salads.

Construction of the Brinton 1704 House was based on recollections of medieval English architecture, resulting in a home of uncommon grace for the 18th century. The house, located in Dilworthtown, Pennsylvania, has been restored to an unusually authentic basis, using room-by-room inventories taken at the time of the builder's death in 1751. Twenty-seven leaded casement windows, plentiful closets, an indoor bake-oven, raised hearths and a colonial herb garden are among the many notable features.

The Nathaniel Newlin Mill, located in Glen Mills, Pennsylvania, is a stone gristmill built in 1704 by Nathaniel Newlin, a Quaker who emigrated from Ireland in 1683. The mill, with its 16-foot wheel, has been restored to working order, offering a fine example of a vital segment of Colonial economic life. The miller's house, built in 1739, is furnished in period. A blacksmith shop, springhouse and log cabin are also part of Newlin Mill Park, which encompasses 150 acres, and includes three miles of nature trails along the millrace and stream.

Blue Cheese Potato Salad

Serves 10 to 12

5 pounds red new potatoes
½ cup dry white wine
Salt and freshly ground black pepper to taste
1¼ cups mayonnaise
1¼ cups sour cream
2½ tablespoons Dijon mustard
2½ tablespoons cider vinegar
½ pound blue cheese, crumbled
5 green onions, minced
1½ cups chopped celery

Place the potatoes in a large pot. Cover with cold water, bring to a boil, and cook until tender. Drain and let cool slightly. Peel the potatoes and cut into 1-inch pieces. Transfer to large bowl. Add the wine and season with salt and pepper, tossing to coat well.

Combine the mayonnaise, sour cream, mustard, vinegar, blue cheese, green onions, and celery in a small bowl. Stir into the potato mixture and adjust the seasonings. Cover and refrigerate up to 1 day ahead. Let stand at room temperature for 30 minutes before serving.

Warm Potato Salad

Serves 4

1 pound small new potatoes, scrubbed
1 tablespoon Dijon mustard
1 tablespoon red wine vinegar
⅓ cup olive oil
2 stalks celery, chopped
½ teaspoon dried rosemary
Salt and freshly ground black pepper to taste

Boil the potatoes in a large pot of boiling water until tender, and then drain. Whisk the mustard and vinegar together in a medium bowl. Slowly drizzle in the olive oil, whisking continuously to emulsify. Stir in the celery and rosemary. Add the potatoes and toss to coat with the dressing. Season with salt and pepper and serve warm.

Pas de Deux ~ **Pasta & Seafood**

Above: Dining Room at N.C. Wyeth House

Right: Terrace Room at Eleutherian Mills, Hagley Museum

Pas de Deux
Pasta & Seafood

The Dining Room of the N.C. Wyeth House in Chadds Ford, Pennsylvania

One of the best-loved illustrators of the 20th century, Newell Convers Wyeth (1882-1945) settled in Chadds Ford in 1908. There, for almost four decades, he gave visual form to some of the most famous characters in literature, enchanting generations of readers. Wyeth was deeply committed to the Brandywine Valley, and throughout his career he painted landscapes that reflect his love of the land, its history and way of life.

In 1926, Wyeth designed the narrow, oak-paneled dining room shown here as part of the renovations to his home on Rocky Hill. The table, also constructed from his design, is set with Carolyn Bockius Wyeth's circa 1915 Copeland Late Spode dinner set. Tours of the N.C. Wyeth House and Studio are offered through the Brandwine River Museum.

Photograph by Heather Hayter and Patsy Keller

Terrace Room at Eleutherian Mills, Hagley Museum

Hagley Museum's Eleutherian Mills is the du Pont family's ancestral home, built by DuPont Company founder Eleuthère Irénée du Pont in 1802. Five generations of the family have lived in the home, most recently Louise Crowninshield, great-granddaughter of E. I. du Pont. Many of the rooms remain decorated in much the same way as Mrs. Crowninshield left them. The terrace room, pictured here, was one of her favorites, and the site of many pleasant Sunday afternoon luncheons. Her love of rustic country accents is evident.

Photograph courtesy of Hagley Museum

Tomato Sauce
(Sauce Tomate, Au Maigre)

Serves 6

¼ **cup extra virgin olive oil**
1 **medium onion, finely diced**
1 **medium carrot, finely diced**
1 **tablespoon garlic, minced**
8 **medium tomatoes, peeled and seeded**
½ **cup tomato purée**
2 **tablespoons chopped fresh basil leaves**
½ **teaspoon salt**
Freshly ground black pepper to taste

Heat the olive oil in a large saucepan on low. Cook the onion, carrot, and garlic until just softened, about 5 minutes; do not brown. Add the tomatoes, tomato purée, basil, salt, and pepper. Cover and simmer about 45 minutes. Pass the sauce through a food mill or process in the food processor. Use immediately or refrigerate and warm through when ready to serve.

♪ *This recipe is different, and very good with any pasta.*

To skin a tomato simply and quickly, spear the stem end with a fork and dip it into a saucepan of boiling water for several seconds. Lift it out, slit the skin with a knife, and peel it off neatly. Remove the seeds by cutting the tomato in half and scooping out the seed cavity with a small spoon.

To keep tomato-based sauces from staining your plastic containers, spray container first with nonstick cooking spray.

Meatballs with Marinara Sauce

Serves 8 to 10

Meatballs

2 pounds ground beef
¾ pound ground pork
2 cups Italian-flavored bread crumbs
4 eggs
1 cup milk
¾ cup chopped fresh parsley leaves
¾ cup freshly grated Parmesan cheese
4 cloves garlic, minced
2 medium onions, chopped
1 tablespoon olive oil

Basic Marinara Sauce

4 tablespoons olive oil
5 cloves garlic, minced
1 small onion, finely chopped (optional)
2 (28 ounce) cans peeled, crushed tomatoes
1 (6 ounce) can tomato paste
4 tablespoons sun-dried tomatoes, chopped
Salt and freshly ground black pepper to taste
10 fresh basil leaves, torn
Freshly grated Parmesan cheese

To prepare the meatballs, combine the ground beef, ground pork, bread crumbs, eggs, milk, parsley, Parmesan, garlic, and onions in a large bowl and mix well. Cover and refrigerate for 30 minutes. Preheat the oven to 350°F. Shape into approximately 25 (3 to 4 inch) meatballs by hand. Heat a large skillet on medium-high and add the oil. Gently sauté the meatballs in the oil until lightly browned. Transfer to a baking pan and bake for 30 minutes.

While the meatballs are baking, prepare the marinara. Using the same sauté pan as the meatballs, heat the oil over medium-high heat. Sauté the garlic and onion, if desired. Add the tomatoes, tomato paste, and sun-dried tomatoes. Bring to a boil, cover, and reduce to a simmer for 30 minutes, stirring occasionally.

Gently place the baked meatballs in the in the marinara (or the sauce of your choice) and cook on medium-low for 1 to 2 hours to allow the flavors to meld. Season with salt and pepper. Serve over pasta and garnish with basil and Parmesan.

Farfalle Olympus

Serves 4

1 cup dehydrated sun-dried tomatoes
6 ounces Farfalle or bowtie pasta, cooked
⅓ cup olive oil
3 large cloves garlic, minced
10 kalamata olives, chopped
¼ teaspoon red pepper flakes
4 ounces goat cheese, crumbled
1 tablespoon pine nuts, toasted
Salt and freshly ground black pepper to taste

To reconstitute the tomatoes, soak them in a bowl of water to cover according to package directions. Drain the softened tomatoes and cut into ¼-inch-thick strips. Cook the pasta in a large pot of boiling, salted water until al dente. While the pasta is cooking, heat a large skillet on medium and add the olive oil. Sauté the garlic for 1 minute; add the tomato, olives, and red pepper. Toss the tomato mixture with the cooked pasta, goat cheese, and pine nuts. Season with salt and pepper, toss again, and serve immediately.

Quick Chicken and Spinach Tetrazzini

Serves 4

4 ounces spaghetti, broken into 3 to 4-inch lengths
1½ cups chopped cooked chicken
1 (9 ounce) package frozen creamed low fat spinach, thawed
1 cup ricotta cheese
½ cup drained, oil-packed sun-dried tomatoes, chopped
5 tablespoons grated Asiago cheese, divided
1 clove garlic, minced
Freshly ground black pepper to taste

Preheat the oven to 500°F. Cook the spaghetti in a large pot of boiling, salted water until al dente. Drain, reserving ¼ cup of the cooking liquid. Combine the spaghetti, chicken, spinach, tomatoes, ricotta, 4 tablespoons of the cheese, the garlic, and reserved cooking liquid in a large bowl. Season with pepper. Spread the mixture in a 9-inch pie plate. Sprinkle with the remaining Asiago cheese. Bake until hot and bubbly, about 15 to 20 minutes.

The town of Lewes, DE, has been a major shipping port since the 1700s. Ships' captains navigated with the help of the lighthouses on Cape May (NJ) and Cape Henlopen (DE). Ocean ships also needed the help of expert river pilots to navigate the shoals and rock ledges in the Delaware River and Bay. The Delaware Bay and River Pilots Association, based in Lewes, continues to provide this important service today, guiding cargo vessels to and from the ports of Wilmington and Philadelphia.

The Delaware Art Museum is renowned for its distinguished 19th and 20th century American art collections, including works from the Pre-Raphaelite period and the Golden Age of American Illustration. The collections include works by Howard Pyle, who trained a generation of equally famous followers: N. C. Wyeth, Frank Schoonover, Stanley Arthyrs, and Maxfield Parrish.

Italian Chicken and Pasta

Serves 4

2 tablespoons olive oil

1 pound boneless, skinless chicken breasts, cut into strips

½ teaspoon salt

¼ teaspoon freshly ground black pepper

1 small onion, cut into eighths

1 teaspoon minced garlic

1 (6 ounce) jar marinated artichoke hearts, undrained, coarsely chopped

1 (7 ounce) jar roasted sweet peppers, undrained, coarsely chopped

½ cup pitted black olives (optional)

½ pound tri-colored fusilli pasta

½ cup freshly grated Parmesan cheese

Heat a large, heavy skillet on medium and add the oil. Season the chicken with the salt and pepper. Sauté the chicken, onion, and garlic until the chicken is cooked through, about 6 minutes, stirring occasionally. Drain. Stir in the artichoke hearts and their juice, the peppers and their juice, and olives, if desired. Reduce the heat to medium-low and cook until heated through, about 6 minutes. Meanwhile, cook the pasta in a large pot of boiling, salted water until al dente. Drain the pasta and transfer to a warmed serving platter. Add the Parmesan cheese and chicken mixture, tossing to distribute evenly. Serve immediately.

Chicken and Sun-Dried Tomatoes over Fettuccine

Serves 4

4 skinless, boneless chicken breast halves

1 (7 ounce) jar sun-dried tomatoes, packed in oil

½ cup chopped onion

2 cloves garlic, minced

2 tablespoons snipped fresh basil leaves or 2 teaspoons dried, crushed

¼ cup sliced ripe black olives

2 tablespoons capers (optional)

2 tablespoons olive oil

½ teaspoon salt

¼ teaspoon freshly ground black pepper

¼ teaspoon crushed red pepper flakes

8 ounces fettuccine

Freshly grated Parmesan cheese

For a professional presentation, top salads or pasta with shavings of dry cheeses such as Parmesan or Asiago, rather than grating the cheese. To make pretty, curvy slivers, draw a vegetable peeler across the edge of the cheese block.

Cut the chicken into ½-inch strips. Drain the sun-dried tomatoes, reserving the oil. Coarsely chop the tomatoes. Heat 1 tablespoon of the reserved oil from the tomatoes in a 12-inch skillet over medium heat. Add the onion and garlic, and cook until tender. Add the chicken and cook about 8 minutes, stirring occasionally, or until the chicken is tender.

Add the basil and tomatoes; cook 1 minute more. Stir in the olives, capers, olive oil, salt, pepper, crushed red pepper, and 2 more tablespoons of the reserved oil from tomatoes; heat through.

Meanwhile, cook the fettuccine in a large pot of boiling, salted water for 8 to 10 minutes, or until al dente. Drain well; return the pasta to the pan. Add the chicken mixture and toss well. Divide among 4 warm serving dishes and sprinkle with Parmesan cheese.

During October and November, the staff at Longwood Gardens strings more than 400,000 Christmas lights, creating a spectacular holiday display. The strings of lights would reach 38.5 miles if stretched end to end.

Lasagna

Serves 8

1 pound ground beef
⅓ pound sausage
1 onion, diced
1 (28 ounce) can whole tomatoes
1 (12 ounce) can tomato paste
1 tablespoon sugar
1½ teaspoon salt
½ teaspoon dried oregano
1 can tomato sauce, preferably Hunt's
½ teaspoon dried thyme
½ teaspoon crushed red pepper
½ teaspoon Italian seasoning
½ teaspoon crushed fresh garlic
2 bay leaves
⅔ (16 ounce) package lasagna noodles
2 eggs
1 (15 ounce) package ricotta cheese
16 ounces mozzarella cheese, shredded

Cook the ground beef, sausage, and onion in a Dutch oven until browned. Drain well and add the tomatoes, tomato paste, sugar, salt, oregano, tomato sauce, thyme, red pepper, Italian seasoning, garlic, and bay leaves. Bring to a boil. Reduce the heat, cover, and simmer at least 30 minutes, preferably longer to allow the flavors to meld. Discard the bay leaves. Cook the noodles in a large pot of boiling, salted water until al dente. Drain, and then arrange half of the noodles in a 13 x 9-inch casserole dish, overlapping to fit.

Preheat the oven to 375°F. Combine the eggs and ricotta in a small bowl. Spoon half over the noodles, sprinkle with half of the mozzarella, and top with half of the sauce. Repeat the layers. Top layer being mozzarella Bake for 45 minutes. Remove from oven and let stand for 10 to 15 minutes before serving.

Cheesy Milano Lasagna Rolls

Serves 10 to 12

Lasagna Rolls

12 lasagna noodles

15 ounces ricotta cheese

4 ounces mozzarella cheese, shredded

¼ cup freshly grated Parmesan cheese

1 (10 ounce) package chopped frozen spinach, thawed and drained well

1 pound bay shrimp, shelled and deveined

1 pound crabmeat, picked through

Salt and freshly ground black pepper to taste

Sauce

4 tablespoons butter

3 tablespoons flour

3 cups half-and-half

⅓ cup chopped onion

¼ cup sherry (optional)

1 heaping tablespoon chopped fresh basil leaves or 1 teaspoon dried

1 heaping tablespoon chopped fresh oregano leaves or 1 teaspoon dried

Salt and freshly ground black pepper to taste

Cook the lasagna noodles in a large pot of boiling, salted water until al dente. Drain and lay out on a work surface. Combine the ricotta, mozzarella, Parmesan, spinach, shrimp, and crab in a medium bowl. Season with salt and pepper. Spread an even layer of filling on each cooked noodle; roll up. Place the rolls in 9 x 11-inch baking pan, seam-side down. (The rolls can be prepared ahead up to this point and refrigerated.)

Preheat the oven to 350°F.

To prepare the sauce, melt the butter in a medium saucepan over medium heat. Whisk in the flour. Add the half-and-half, onion, sherry, basil, and oregano and simmer until reduced and slightly thickened. Season with salt and pepper. Pour the sauce over the rolls and bake for 20 to 25 minutes (or slightly longer if refrigerated first). Serve with hot sourdough bread and a fresh green salad.

During the Revolutionary War, the British fleet lay anchored off New Castle (the original capital), which forced the Delaware assembly to retreat inland to Dover. The assembly met at various sites over the next few years. Then, in 1781~ the same year that Continental forces defeated the British at Yorktown, effectively ending the Revolution ~ Delaware delegates officially agreed to make centrally located Dover the state's new capital.

Olive Oil

In 1682, William Penn declared that Cape Henlopen would be for, "the usage of the citizens of Lewes and Sussex County," making it one of the first public lands established in the United States. A lighthouse was constructed in 1765, which collapsed in 1926.

Olive oils are great for cooking and salad dressings, and are available in several grades. The lower the acidity, the higher the quality of the oil:

~ **"Extra Virgin"** means the first oil from the first press. It has the best flavor, color and aroma, and is the most expensive. Use it when you want the full flavor of the oil to come through, but don't waste it on frying. It's wonderful for salad dressings, drizzled over steamed vegetables, served on pasta, or for dipping crusty bread.

~ **"Fine Virgin"** olive oil is from the same pressing, but is slightly less flavorful and more acidic. It can be used in the same manner as extra virgin oil, but is also wonderful for sautéing, when you want the flavor of the oil to enhance a dish.

~ **"Pure"** olive oil is a low-cost blend of refined and virgin oils. While not as flavorful as the higher grades, it is useful for sautéing and simple marinades when the olive flavor is not as important.

~ **"Light"** or **"Lite"** olive oil is generally the lowest quality, extracted by heat after the better quality "cold press" oil has been removed from the olives. Although this oil is flavorless, and typically sold for greatly reduced prices on the world markets, in the U.S. it is sold as "light" for a premium price. The "light" designation refers to flavor, not calories, as all olive oil has the same number of calories per tablespoon.

Olive oils should be stored in a cool, dark place at room temperature. Keep only a small amount near the stove for cooking, as the heat will cause it to spoil. Olive oil is more perishable than some other oils. It will keep for longer periods in the refrigerator, however this will cause it to solidify, so it will need to be warmed gently before use. Never use oil without smelling it first, since a drop or two of rancid oil can ruin a dish.

To judge the quality of an olive oil, simply dip a piece of French bread into the oil and taste it. Once you have tested a variety of oils in this manner, you will know which ones you prefer.

Seashell Provolone Casserole

Serves 10 to 12

¼ cup butter, melted
3 medium onions, finely chopped
1½ to 2 pounds ground beef
1 (15½ ounce) jar plain spaghetti sauce
1 (16 ounce) can stewed tomatoes, drained
1 (4 ounce) can mushroom stems and pieces, drained
1 teaspoon garlic salt
1 (16 ounce) package seashell macaroni
8 ounces provolone cheese, grated
2 cups sour cream
4 ounces mozzarella cheese, grated

Preheat the oven to 350°F. Heat a large skillet on medium-high and melt the butter. Sauté the onion until just tender. Add the ground beef and cook until browned, stirring to crumble the meat. Stir in the spaghetti sauce, tomatoes, mushrooms, and garlic salt. Bring to a simmer and cook for 20 minutes. Cook the macaroni in a large pot of boiling, lightly salted water until al dente. (Use no more than 1½ teaspoons of salt.) Drain. Place half of the macaroni in a deep, 4-quart greased casserole, layer with half of the provolone cheese, then half of the sour cream, and half of the meat sauce. Repeat the layers, and then finish with the mozzarella cheese on top. Cover and bake for 30 minutes; uncover and bake for another 15 minutes. The casserole can be prepared in advance, chilled or frozen, and baked immediately before serving.

Cape Henlopen State Park boasts an 80-foot sand dune, which is the highest dune between Cape Cod and Cape Hatteras.

Rehoboth Beach's name comes from a biblical term meaning "room enough." The town was originally constructed by Methodists, who purchased the land for a summer camp and meeting place. Rehoboth Beach is now the state's largest coastal resort town.

Seafood Risotto

Serves 4 to 6

4½ cups fish or shellfish broth
3 tablespoons butter, divided
2 cloves garlic, chopped
¾ pound seafood, such as shrimp, lobster, crabmeat, scallops, or combination, shelled, deveined, and cut into bite-size pieces
1 tablespoon olive oil
3 to 4 chopped green onions
1½ cups Arborio rice (do not substitute)
½ cup dry white wine
2 plum tomatoes, chopped
¼ cup chopped fresh parsley leaves
⅓ cup light cream
Salt to taste

For a successful finished product, be sure to prep all ingredients before beginning to cook.

Bring the broth to a simmer in a small saucepan. Melt 1 tablespoon of the butter in a large skillet over medium heat. Sauté the garlic until golden. Add the seafood and sauté for 2 to 3 minutes, or until no longer transparent. Do not overcook. Remove from the heat and set aside.

Heat a large saucepan on medium-high and add the olive oil and remaining 2 tablespoons of butter. Sauté the green onions briefly. Add the rice, stirring to coat well. Add the wine and stir until completely absorbed. Add the broth, ½ cup at a time, stirring frequently. Adjust the heat so that each addition continues to simmer and is completely absorbed in about 2 minutes. (The broth is completely absorbed when a wooden spoon scraping the bottom of the pan leaves a clear trail.) Keep stirring to prevent sticking.

When you add the last ½ cup of broth, also add the seafood, tomatoes, and parsley, and continue to stir until the broth is mostly absorbed. Add the cream, stir to mix well, and season with salt to taste. Remove from the heat and serve immediately.

Scallop Sauté
Serves 4

1 pound sea scallops
¼ cup flour
2 tablespoons butter
2 tablespoons olive oil
1 tomato, coarsely diced
1 tablespoon chopped fresh parsley
1 tablespoon freshly squeezed lemon juice
¼ teaspoon garlic powder
Lemon wedges, for garnish

Lightly dust the scallops with the flour and shake off any excess. Heat a large skillet on medium-high and add the butter and oil. Sauté the scallops until golden brown, being careful not to over-cook. Add the tomato, parsley, lemon juice, and garlic. Cook until the tomato is heated through and the scallops are tender. Serve with lemon wedges.

Linguine with Clam Sauce
Serves 8

1 pound linguine
2 to 3 tablespoons olive oil
10 cloves garlic, slivered
3 (6 to 8 ounce) cans chopped clams, with juice
1 bottle clam juice
1 tablespoon chopped fresh oregano leaves, or more to taste
Freshly grated Parmesan or Asiago cheese to taste
Salt and freshly ground black pepper to taste

Cook the linguine in a large pot of boiling, salted water until al dente. While the pasta is cooking, heat a large pan on medium and add the oil. Sauté the garlic until golden. Add the clams and clam juice. Simmer 5 to 10 minutes, and then add the oregano. Simmer another 5 minutes, or until reduced to the desired consistency. Add the cooked linguine to the clam sauce, sprinkle in the cheese, adjust the seasonings, and toss thoroughly to combine. Serve immediately in warm pasta bowls.

On December 3, 1787, Delaware's 30 representatives to the Constitutional Convention gathered in Dover's Golden Fleece Tavern for a crucial meeting, while construction continued on a new state house across Dover Green. Just four days later, on December 7, 1787, they voted unanimously to approve the fledgling nation's new Federal Constitution. They had already battled to ensure that all states, regardless of size, would receive equal representation in the central government. Now, by being first to ratify the Constitution, Delaware would forever be known as "The First State."

In 1981, the Delaware Legislature adopted the weakfish ~ also known as sea trout, yellow-fin trout, squeteague and tiderunner~ as Delaware's State Fish. This was in recognition of the weakfish's value as a game and food fish, as well as sportfishing's overall recreational and economic contribution to the state.

Pasta with Lobster and Tarragon

Serves 6 as first course, 4 as main course

2 tablespoons extra virgin olive oil
½ cup finely chopped yellow onion
1 (28 ounce) can Italian plum tomatoes, drained and chopped
2 teaspoons dried tarragon
Salt and freshly ground black pepper to taste
1 cup heavy cream
Pinch of cayenne pepper
1½ pounds cooked lobster meat (about 4 cups) (steaming frozen tails works well)
1 pound spaghetti or spinach fettuccine
Sprigs of fresh parsley, basil, or tarragon, for garnish

Heat a large skillet on medium-high and add the oil. Add the onion, reduce the heat to medium, and cook until tender. Stir in the tomatoes and tarragon, season with salt and pepper, and bring to a boil. Reduce the heat, cover, and simmer for 30 minutes, stirring occasionally.

Stir in the heavy cream. Simmer another 15 minutes, or until slightly reduced, stirring frequently. Adjust the seasonings. Stir in the cayenne and lobster meat. Simmer another 5 minutes, or just until the lobster is heated through.

While the sauce is cooking, cook the spaghetti in a large pot of boiling, salted water until al dente. Drain and immediately arrange on warm serving plates. Spoon sauce evenly over the pasta and garnish with a sprig of fresh herbs. Serve with crusty French bread and a green salad.

Stir-Fried Curried Pasta with Spinach and Scallops

Serves 4 to 6

1 pound medium-size pasta shells
½ cup non-fat yogurt
¼ cup defatted homemade or reduced-sodium canned chicken stock
1 tablespoon vegetable oil
6 scallions, trimmed and thinly sliced (about 1 cup)
4 teaspoons peeled and minced fresh ginger
4 teaspoons curry powder
2 cloves garlic, minced
1 pound bay scallops
10 ounces fresh spinach, washed thoroughly and shredded
8 medium-size plum tomatoes, seeded and diced (about 2 cups)
Salt to taste

Cook the pasta in a large pot of boiling, salted water for 10 to 15 minutes until al dente. Drain and rinse under cold water until cooled. Whisk together the yogurt and chicken stock in a small bowl. Prep each remaining ingredient for fast and accurate stir-frying.

Heat a wok or heavy sauté pan on high. Heat the oil until almost smoking. Add the scallions, ginger, curry powder, and garlic, and stir-fry 10 second until fragrant. Add the scallops and stir-fry for 2 minutes, or until opaque. Add the spinach and stir-fry for 1 minute, until just wilted but still bright green. Add the tomatoes and reserved shells, and toss until evenly distributed. Add the reserved yogurt mixture and toss again. Cover and cook for 30 seconds until heated through. Season with salt, as needed. Serve immediately.

When is a crab not a crab? When it's a horseshoe crab! The Delaware Bay is home to the world's largest population of horseshoe crabs, of which only four species exist in the world. They are one of the oldest creatures on earth ~ they were here 100 million years before the dinosaur.

Each spring, 1.5 million migrating shorebirds, including some endangered species, fly non-stop for thousands of miles from South America to the Delaware Bay area. En route to their Arctic breeding grounds, these birds arrive here well below normal body weight. Each will each consume over 8,000 horseshoe crab eggs per day during their three-week visit.

Grilled Clam Bake

Serves 4

4 (12 x 18 inch) sheets heavy-duty aluminum foil
4 chicken breasts, split
4 small red skin potatoes, scrubbed
2 ears of corn, husked and cut in half
1 dozen little neck clams, scrubbed clean
3 tablespoons butter, thinly sliced
½ pound hot Italian sausage, cut into 3-inch slices (optional)
Salt and freshly ground black pepper to taste
Paprika to taste
4 tablespoons water, divided

Spray sheets of aluminum foil with nonstick cooking spray. Center the chicken, breast-side up, on the foil. Place a potato, ½ ear of corn, 3 clams and 2 sausage slices, if desired, over the chicken breast. Dot with butter and season with salt, pepper, and paprika. Drizzle packet ingredients with 1 tablespoon of water. Seal each packet well, doubling at each fold.

Prepare grill to medium-high heat. Place each packet on grill, seal-side up. Turn packets with tongs after 30 minutes; cook additional 15 minutes. When ready to serve, slit packets carefully to allow steam to escape before opening fully.

If desired, packets may be placed on a baking sheet and baked for 1 hour, without turning, in a 375° oven. Follow same procedure for opening packets.

Mussels in a Red Thai Curry Sauce

Serves 6 as a first course

¼ cup butter

5 plum tomatoes, seeded and chopped

2 tablespoons minced garlic

1 tablespoon peeled and minced fresh ginger

2 (14 ounce) cans unsweetened coconut milk

1 tablespoon Thai red curry paste

¼ cup plus 3 tablespoons chopped fresh cilantro leaves, divided

1 teaspoon salt

3 pounds mussels, scrubbed and debearded

Heat a large, heavy pot on medium-high and melt the butter. Add the tomatoes, garlic, and ginger; sauté until the garlic is tender, about 2 minutes. Stir in the coconut milk, curry paste, ¼ cup of the cilantro, and the salt. Simmer for 4 minutes to blend the flavors. Add the mussels; cover and cook until mussels open, about 5 minutes. Discard any mussels that do not open. Pour the mussels and the cooking juices into a warm serving bowl. Garnish with the remaining chopped cilantro. Serve with hot, crusty bread.

Summer Salmon with Mango Salsa

Serves 2

1 (10 ounce) mango, peeled, pitted, chopped

¼ cup chopped fresh cilantro leaves

¼ cup chopped red onion

1 tablespoon freshly squeezed lime juice

1 clove garlic, finely chopped

2 teaspoons minced seeded jalapeño

2 tablespoons olive oil, divided

Salt and freshly ground black pepper to taste

2 (6 ounce) pieces of salmon

Prepare the grill or preheat the broiler. Combine the mango, cilantro, red onion, lime juice, garlic, and jalapeño in small bowl; stir in 1½ tablespoons of the oil. Season the salsa with salt and pepper. Brush the salmon with the remaining ½ tablespoon of oil. Grill or broil salmon until just opaque in center, about 4 to 5 minutes per side. Serve with the salsa.

Lewes, Delaware, was named for the county seat of Sussex, England. The town serves as a gateway to the New Jersey coast, via the Cape May - Lewes Ferry, which makes regular 70-minute trips across 17 miles of Delaware Bay.

The Delaware Breakwater at Cape Henlopen State Park was the first structure of its kind in the western hemisphere.

Sesame-Lime Salmon

Serves 2

½ cup of rice vinegar
½ cup freshly squeezed lime juice
¼ cup sesame oil
¼ cup canola oil
¾ pound salmon or shrimp
Salt and freshly ground black pepper to taste
Lime wedges

Combine the rice vinegar, lime juice, sesame oil, and canola oil in a small bowl. Place the fish or shrimp in a large glass baking dish. Pour the marinade over the fish. Season with salt and pepper. Cover and chill 2 to 3 hours to marinate. Prepare the grill, and grill the salmon to the desired doneness. Garnish with lime.

Salmon with Dill Sauce

Serves 4

1 tablespoon butter or margarine
½ cup chopped green onions
1 (10¾ ounce) can cream of chicken soup
½ cup cream
2 tablespoons white wine
2 tablespoon chopped fresh dill leaves or 1 teaspoon dried, plus additional for garnish
4 salmon steaks

Heat a large sauté pan on medium and melt the butter. Add the onions and cook until tender. Add the soup, cream, wine, and dill, stirring until smooth. Place the salmon steak in the pan and bring to a boil. Cover, reduce the heat to low, and simmer for 15 minutes, or until the steaks are just poached through. Serve the salmon on warm plates and spoon with some of the sauce. Garnish with fresh dill, if desired.

Tuna with Sesame-Peppercorn Crust

Serves 4

1 tablespoon 4-peppercorn spice mix, a blend of black, white, pink, and green whole peppercorns
¼ cup sesame seeds
1 lemon, quartered
4 (6 to 7 ounce) tuna steaks
Dried dill, for seasoning
Garlic powder, for seasoning
2 tablespoons butter

Preheat the oven to 350°F. Lightly grease a large baking sheet. Combine the peppercorn mix and sesame seeds in a plastic zipperlock bag. Crush with a mallet. Squeeze the juice from the lemon quarters onto both sides of the tuna. Season both sides of the tuna with the dill, garlic powder, peppercorn mixture, and salt. Arrange the tuna on the prepared baking sheet. Dot with the butter. Bake until the fish is cooked to the desired degree of doneness, about 10 to 15 minutes for medium, depending on the thickness of the steaks. Serve on warm plates.

Melt together equal portions of butter and Roquefort cheese to make a tasty sauce for steak or fish.

Shrimp Scampi

Serves 6

2 pounds large fresh shrimp, peeled and deveined
1 cup butter, melted
¼ cup olive oil
1 tablespoon dried parsley flakes
1 tablespoon freshly squeezed lemon juice
¾ teaspoon salt
¾ teaspoon garlic powder
¾ teaspoon dried basil
½ teaspoon dried oregano
Freshly grated Parmesan cheese, for garnish

Preheat the oven to 450°F. Place the shrimp in a single layer in a 10 x 15-inch jelly-roll pan. Combine the butter, olive oil, parsley, lemon juice, salt, garlic powder, basil, and oregano in a small bowl and pour over the shrimp. Bake for 4 minutes, or until the shrimp are pink. Serve over cooked pasta and garnish with freshly grated Parmesan cheese.

Pas de Deux

On August 1, 1859,
the Fenwick Island
Lighthouse cast its first
shaft of light, which could
be seen for 15 miles out over
the dangerous shoals. The
design of the lighthouse is
somewhat unusual: It has two
brick towers instead of one.
Paul Pepper and his wife
Dorothy cared for the
lighthouse for years, and Paul
was the founder of the Friends of
the Fenwick Island Lighthouse,
Inc. In 1999, the state of
Delaware renovated the lighthouse for all to enjoy.

Sautéed Chilean Sea Bass

Serves 6

1 cup all-purpose flour
Salt and freshly ground black pepper
1½ pounds Chilean sea bass fillets
3 tablespoons butter, divided
2 tablespoons olive oil
1 cup dry white wine
2 tablespoons drained capers

Place the flour in a shallow bowl. Season with salt and pepper.
Dredge each fillet in the flour, shaking off any excess. Heat a large
skillet on medium for 3 to 4 minutes. Add the 2 tablespoons of the
butter and the olive oil. Increase the heat to high and sauté the
fillets in batches, shaking the pan occasionally until the bottom of
the fish is nicely browned, about 3 minutes. Turn and brown the
other side. Remove the fish to a serving platter and keep warm.
Repeat with the remaining fillets. (Unlike many fish, sea bass tastes
best when cooked all the way through.) Deglaze the pan with the
white wine, scraping the bottom of the pan to release any browned
bits and stirring over high heat until reduced by about ⅓. Stir in
the remaining butter and drained capers. Drizzle the sauce around
each fillet.

Grilled or Broiled Marinated Swordfish

Serves 8

Marinade

1 cup vegetable oil
Juice of 2 lemons
2 tablespoons white wine vinegar
½ to ⅓ teaspoon salt
⅛ teaspoon freshly ground black pepper
½ teaspoon dried basil or 1 teaspoon chopped fresh basil leaves
Small pinch of cayenne pepper
1 medium clove garlic, minced

Fish

8 swordfish steaks, about ⅓ pound each
Melted butter, for garnish
Lemon wedges, for garnish

Combine all the marinade ingredients in a medium glass bowl. Add the fish pieces and marinate at least 4 hours in the refrigerator, turning several times. Prepare the grill or preheat the broiler. Remove the fish from the marinade and pat dry. Grill 6 to 7 minutes on each side, or until the fish begins to flake when tested with a fork. Alternatively, broil about 4 inches from the heat in the oven. Drizzle the cooked fish with some melted butter and serve with lemon wedges.

Quaker Hill Historic District was home to Thomas Garrett, a conductor of the "Underground Railroad." Wilmington was the "last stop to freedom" on this historic road. Quaker Hill is also the home to John Dickinson, a signer of the constitution. The area has excellent examples of architecture dating back to 1738. It is located at 4th Street between Washington and West Streets in Wilmington. The Quaker Meeting House there is still in use.

For a tasty, low-fat alternative, substitute chicken broth for butter when browning onions, garlic, or other vegetables.

Sweet-and-Sour Swordfish

Serves 8

2 teaspoons olive oil
3 large onions, thinly sliced
2 cloves garlic, minced
Pinch of hot pepper flakes
¼ cup raisins
2 teaspoons sugar
¼ cup balsamic vinegar
¼ cup dry white wine
Salt to taste
8 (4 ounce) swordfish steaks, about 1 inch thick

Preheat the oven to 425°F. Heat a large skillet on medium-high and add the oil. Sauté the onions and garlic, and sprinkle in the hot pepper flakes, raisins, and sugar. Cook until the onions begin to brown. Add the balsamic vinegar, wine, and salt. Continue cooking until the onions are very limp and tender and the juices almost disappear. Pat the swordfish dry. Place in baking dish and the spoon onion mixture over top. Bake for 18 to 20 minutes, depending on thickness of fish, until just cooked through.

Catfish Creole

Serves 4

2 tablespoons olive oil
1 large green bell pepper, cut into 1-inch pieces
1 large onion, cut into 1-inch pieces
1 (28 ounce) can chopped plum tomatoes, liquid reserved
¼ cup white wine Worcestershire sauce
1 tablespoon Worcestershire sauce
2 teaspoons seasoned salt, preferably Lawry's
2 teaspoons chicken bouillon granules
1 teaspoon sugar
½ teaspoon freshly ground black pepper
1 pound farm raised catfish fillets, trimmed of fat and cut into bite-size pieces

Heat a large skillet on medium-high and add the oil. Sauté the green pepper and onion just until limp. Add the plum tomatoes and their liquid. Stir in the Worcestershire sauces, seasoned salt, bouillon, sugar, and pepper. Simmer for 5 minutes. Add the fish and simmer another 5 to 10 minutes, depending on thickness of fish. Ladle over cooked rice and serve with Italian bread toasted with garlic butter.

Shrimp in Mango Cream

Serves 4

Seasoning Mix

1 teaspoon coriander

1 teaspoon onion powder

1 teaspoon freshly ground black pepper

1 teaspoon dried ancho chile peppers

1 teaspoon salt

¾ teaspoon cayenne pepper

¾ teaspoon ground cinnamon

¾ teaspoon garlic powder

¾ teaspoon white pepper

½ teaspoon ground cloves

½ teaspoon ground nutmeg

Shrimp

2 medium-size ripe mangoes, peeled and pitted

8 tablespoons unsalted butter

3 cups heavy cream

1 pound peeled, deveined shrimp

Combine the seasoning ingredients in a small bowl. Purée the mangoes in a blender and set aside. Heat the butter in a 4 or 5-quart pot over high heat. Add the seasoning mix and stir until the butter melts. Stir in the cream and cook, whisking constantly to make for a light and fluffy sauce, until the mixture just begins to boil. Stir in the shrimp. As soon as the shrimp begin to turn opaque and bubbles appear around the edges of the pot, add the mango purée. Stir constantly and bring the mixture to a full boil. Remove from the heat and serve immediately over rice or pasta in warm dishes.

The only place you find success before work is in the dictionary.

~ May V. Smith

Bell music was part of
founder Pierre du Pont's
original vision of Longwood
Gardens. In 1929, he had a
61-foot tall stone Chimes
Tower constructed next to
the waterfall adjoining the
Main Fountain Garden.
Twenty-five tubular chimes
were installed, which rang for
the first time on April 20, 1930.
In 1956, two years after
Mr. du Pont's death, the
original chimes were replaced
with a 32-note electronic
carillon. This sounded the
quarter hours, and had played
16,600 concerts by 1981,
when the bells deteriorated
to the point that they were
no longer playable.

Shrimp Newburg

Serves 8

2 pounds fresh or frozen shrimp, cooked and shelled
¼ cup sherry
¼ cup cooking oil
3 tablespoons flour
¾ teaspoon salt
Dash of cayenne pepper
Dash of nutmeg
1½ cups heavy cream
1 egg yolk, beaten

Wash the shrimp in cold water, drain, and place in a medium
bowl. Pour the sherry over the shrimp, tossing to coat. Combine
the oil, flour, salt, cayenne pepper, and nutmeg in heavy saucepan
over medium heat. Reduce the heat to medium-low and slowly
add the cream, stirring continuously, until the mixture thickens
and boils. Stir a little of the sauce into the egg yolk to temper the
egg, and then stir into the sauce. Add the shrimp and sherry. Cook
2 minutes, or until the shrimp is just warmed through. Serve over
toast or rice.

♪ *This is a family favorite that is often requested for special occasions.*

Shrimp Étouffée

Serves 6

1 cup flour

1 cup vegetable oil

3 cups chopped onion

1 green bell pepper, chopped

2 stalks celery, chopped

4 tablespoons chile powder, or more to taste

1 tablespoon cayenne pepper, or more to taste

2 teaspoons dried oregano

1 teaspoon dried basil

1 teaspoon crushed red pepper flakes

2 cloves garlic, crushed

¼ cup Worcestershire sauce

¼ cup sherry

1 cup chicken stock

3 or 4 (14½ ounce) cans diced tomatoes

12 drops Tabasco sauce, or more to taste

Salt and freshly ground black pepper to taste

1½ pounds shrimp, peeled and deveined

Filé powder, for sprinkling (optional)

Cook the flour and oil over medium-high heat to make a roux. Stir continuously until the color of peanut butter. Add the onions, green pepper, and celery, stirring until the onions are limp. Add the chile powder, cayenne, oregano, basil, red pepper, and garlic. Stir for 1 minute. Add the Worcestershire, sherry, chicken stock, tomatoes, and Tabasco. Stir well, reduce the heat to low, and simmer for 10 to 15 minutes, until the flavors blend. Stir frequently to make sure the sauce does not stick to the pan. Check the seasoning and adjust as necessary. Add the raw shrimp; increase the heat and simmer until the shrimp is pink. Continue to simmer an additional 15 minutes to let the flavors meld. Serve with white rice and sprinkle filé powder on top just before serving, if desired.

For a delicious non-seafood dish, replace the shrimp with 3 to 4 cups cubed, cooked chicken.

On Memorial Day, 2001, the inaugural concert was held for a new 62-bell carillon at Longwood Gardens. It has more bells than any other carillon in Pennsylvania. The largest bell is almost 6 feet in diameter, and weighs 6,908 pounds; the smallest is only 6 inches across, and weighs 20 pounds. The bells were custom-made in the Netherlands, and transported by boat to New York. The 55,000-pound instrument was assembled on the ground by Dutch and American craftsmen, then lifted as one piece into the temporarily roofless Chimes Tower, by a 275-ton crane. The 5-octave carillon can be played by hand from a traditional baton keyboard, or automatically by a unique touch-sensitive computer system.

Notes

Swing Time ~ **Entrées**

**Above: Dining Room at
George Read II House**

**Right: Dining Room at the
Nemours Mansion**

Swing Time
Entrées

Dining Room at the George Reed II House

The Strand, in New Castle, Delaware, is lined with picturesque Georgian houses, foremost of which is the George Read II House. The Read House was built in 1801 by George Read II, son of one of the signers of the Declaration of Independence. The interior reflects the height of Federal grandeur, featuring elaborately carved woodwork, relief plasterwork, and gilded fanlights. The dining room was redecorated circa 1920 by the Lairds, the third family to reside in the house. The walls are decorated with hand-painted wallpaper depicting scenes of New Castle. The table dates from circa 1825, in the style of Duncan Phyfe, and the place settings were designed by Tiffany. The Read House is operated as a museum by the Historical Society of Delaware.

Photograph by Jim Bader, courtesy of the Historical Society of Delaware

Dining Room at the Nemours Mansion

The Nemours Mansion in Wilmington is known as "the Versailles of the Brandywine Valley." An outstanding feature of the dining room is the Louis XV cut glass and crystal chandelier. It is thought to have come from the Schönbrunn Palace outside Vienna, Austria, where Marie Antoinette spent her childhood. Marie Antoinette became the wife of King Louis XVI, whose portrait is above the fireplace. Pierre Samuel du Pont, who was the great-great-grandfather of Alfred I. du Pont, was an economic advisor to Louis XVI. The carpet is a rare Sarouk. The dining table is set with decorative gold-banded Moser crystal, embedded with the du Pont coat of arms. English Coalport plates with gilt rims sit beneath English Derby Imari china plates. Matching Imari serving pieces are on the table, also.

Photograph courtesy of The Nemours Foundation

Chicken Cordon Bleu

Serves 8

Chicken

4 whole skinless, boneless chicken breasts, cut in half and trimmed of fat
8 to 10 thin slice deli ham, thinly sliced
10 slices sharp white Cheddar cheese
1 cup flour
Salt and freshly ground black pepper to taste
3 eggs
3 tablespoons water
1 to 2 tablespoons oil, for sautéing

Sauce

2 tablespoons butter
1 (10 ounce) carton fresh mushrooms, sliced
¼ cup chopped onion
1 (10¾ ounce) can cream of mushroom soup
Milk, for thinning
Salt and freshly ground black pepper taste
2 to 3 tablespoons sherry

Place the chicken breasts between 2 sheets of plastic wrap and pound lightly to an even thickness. In the center of each breast, place 1 slice of ham and 1 slice of cheese. Roll up each chicken breast and secure with toothpicks. Season the flour generously with salt and pepper on a plate. Beat the eggs and water together in a medium bowl. Dredge each breast in the seasoned flour, dip in the egg wash, and then dredge in the flour again. Heat a large pan on medium-high. Add the oil and sauté the chicken rolls until just golden brown. Place the browned chicken in a small ovenproof casserole dish.

Preheat the oven to 350°F. To prepare the sauce, heat a large pan on medium-high and add the butter. Sauté the mushrooms and onion until soft. Stir in the mushroom soup and cook until bubbly. Add enough milk until desired consistency is attained. Season with salt and pepper. Stir in the sherry and cook until bubbly. Pour the sauce over the chicken and bake for 30 to 35 minutes. Serve hot over rice or pasta.

The Delaware state bird is the Blue Hen Chicken. During the Revolutionary War, the men of Delaware's First Regiment, who were recruited in Kent County, took with them gamecocks that were renowned for their fighting ability. The men, who valiantly fought in almost every major battle, were subsequently nicknamed the "Blue Hens." The chicken has become an ideal symbol for the state, as nearly 70% of Delaware's agricultural income is derived from the poultry industry. The Blue Hens (athletic teams) now fight for the University of Delaware.

Woodburn Mansion, in Dover, has served as the official residence of the governor since 1965. The Georgian-style home dates to 1790, and its grounds feature carefully restored parterre boxwood plantings, as well as a reflecting pool and several unusual trees. Among these is a Giant Sequoia, presented as a gift to Delaware by Ronald Reagan, when he was governor of California. Woodburn was also once a legendary station on the Underground Railroad.

Chicken with Tomato and Basil

Serves 6

6 skinless, boneless chicken breast halves, trimmed
2 eggs, beaten
1 cup Italian-seasoned bread crumbs
½ cup olive oil, divided
Freshly grated Parmesan cheese
1 cup chopped onion
1 clove garlic, mined
1½ pounds tomatoes, chopped
½ cup snipped fresh basil leaves
½ teaspoon sugar
Salt and freshly ground black pepper to taste

Soak the chicken breasts in the beaten eggs in the refrigerator for 2 to 3 hours. Remove the chicken and roll in the bread crumbs. Preheat the oven to 350°F. Heat ¼ cup of the olive oil in a 12-inch skillet. Cook the chicken, uncovered, over medium heat for 5 to 7 minutes per side, or until lightly browned. Place in a shallow baking dish. Bake about 20 minutes, or until tender. Sprinkle generously with Parmesan cheese.

While the chicken is baking, prepare the sauce. Heat a 2-quart saucepan on medium-high and add the remaining ¼ cup of olive oil. Cook the onion and garlic until tender. Add the tomatoes, basil, sugar, salt, and pepper. Bring to a boil and cook over medium-high heat for 2 to 3 minutes. Reduce the heat to medium-low and cook for 20 minutes more. Serve the sauce over the chicken.

Glazed Chicken

Serves 4

2½ pounds skinless chicken breasts, bone-in

⅓ cup molasses

3 tablespoons cider vinegar

1 tablespoon Worcestershire sauce

1 tablespoon Dijon mustard

½ teaspoon Tabasco sauce

1 teaspoon freshly ground black pepper

½ teaspoon salt

Place the chicken in single layer in a baking dish. Combine the remaining ingredients in a small bowl and stir until evenly mixed. Pour the sauce over the chicken, cover, and refrigerate overnight. Preheat the oven to 375°F. Bake the chicken for 30 minutes, or until the juices run clear.

Grilled Sesame Chicken

Serves 4 to 6

Marinade

½ cup olive oil

½ cup white wine

½ cup soy sauce

4 cloves garlic, crushed

3 tablespoons sesame seeds

1 to 2 tablespoons peeled and grated fresh ginger

1 tablespoon dry mustard

1 teaspoon freshly ground black pepper

½ cup chopped green onions

2 whole chickens, quartered

Combine all the marinade ingredients in a medium bowl. Place the chicken in large, plastic zipperlock bag and pour in the marinade, squeezing out the air to seal. Marinate in the refrigerator for 4 to 8 hours, turning occasionally. Prepare the grill to a medium heat. Remove the chicken, reserving the marinade, and pat dry. Grill for 15 to 20 minutes, basting frequently with the marinade.

During WWII, secret rocket development took place in the building complex that included Hanger 1301, at what was then known as Dover Army Airfield. From the 1950s to the 1970s, various fighter squadrons called the hanger home. In the 1990s, after restoration and placement on the National Register of Historic Places, Hanger 1301 was given new life as the home of The Air Mobility Command Museum. The AMC Museum preserves and displays the history of the Air Mobility Command and Dover Air Force Base. Visitors see aviation history come alive, from bi-planes and bombers to giant C-5 cargo jets.

Hoisin Chicken Skewers

Serves 4

½ cup hoisin sauce
2 tablespoon peeled and minced fresh ginger
2 tablespoon oriental sesame oil
2 tablespoon rice vinegar
4 chicken breast halves, cut into 1-inch cubes
Salt and freshly ground black pepper to taste
2 tablespoon sesame seeds

Prepare the grill.

Whisk together the hoisin sauce, ginger, sesame oil, and rice vinegar in a medium bowl. Set aside 4 tablespoons of the sauce for glazing. Stir the chicken into the remaining sauce and let stand for 10 minutes.

Thread the chicken onto 8 skewers, spacing pieces ½ inch apart to allow thorough cooking. Season with salt and pepper. Grill the chicken until cooked through and slightly charred, brushing with the reserved glaze and turning often, about 8 minutes. Remove the skewers from grill and sprinkle with sesame seeds.

Spicy Chicken, Broccoli and Nuts

Serves 4

Béchamel Sauce

2 tablespoons butter
2 tablespoons flour
Salt and freshly ground black pepper to taste
1 cup half-and-half, whole milk, or low-fat milk

Spicy Chicken

2 cups broccoli florets
2 tablespoons oil
Green or red Thai curry paste, or other hot sauce to taste (optional)
12 ounces chicken strips
2 tablespoons sugar
¼ cup sun-dried tomatoes
1 tablespoon chili powder
½ teaspoon ground ginger
½ teaspoon cayenne pepper
½ teaspoon turmeric
2 tablespoons chopped fresh cilantro leaves
Salt to taste
2 tablespoons soy sauce
¼ cup low-fat peanut butter
¼ cup roasted peanuts or cashews

To prepare the béchamel, melt the butter in a medium saucepan over medium heat. Stir in the flour, salt, and pepper. Slowly add the half-and-half, whisking continuously.

To prepare the chicken dish, blanch the broccoli in a large pot of boiling water until crisp-tender. Drain and rinse under cold water. Heat a large sauté pan on medium-high and add the oil. Add the curry paste, if desired, and cook for 2 minutes. Add the chicken, sugar, sun-dried tomatoes, chile powder, ginger, cayenne, turmeric, cilantro, and salt. Sauté until the chicken is almost cooked through, and then add the soy sauce. Pour in the béchamel sauce and blend in the peanut butter, stirring to warm through. Add the nuts and broccoli, cooking until the broccoli is warmed through. Serve immediately over hot rice, lo mein, or egg noodles.

Thai curry pastes are pungent flavor enhancers, available in many Oriental food markets. Color indicates their strength:

- *Red - made with red chiles, very hot*

- *Green - green chiles, hot and spicy*

- *Orange - sour, made with rice vinegar*

- *Yellow - like the red, but with a stronger curry flavor*

*Sussex County
Delaware, birthplace
of the broiler chicken
industry, produces more
than 200 million chickens
annually, nearly twice as
many as any other county
in the U.S. Since Delaware
has fewer than one million
residents, the ratio of
chickens to Delawareans
is approximately
250 to 1.*

Overnight Chicken

Serves 10

10 pieces boneless, skinless chicken
1 head garlic, peeled and finely chopped
¼ cup dried oregano
Salt and freshly ground black pepper to taste
½ cup red wine vinegar
½ cup olive oil
1 cup pitted prunes
½ cup pitted Spanish green olives
½ cup capers with a bit of juice
6 bay leaves
1 cup packed light brown sugar
1 cup white wine
¼ cup chopped fresh Italian parsley or cilantro leaves

Combine the chicken, garlic, oregano, salt, pepper, vinegar, olive oil, prunes, olives, capers and juice, and bay leaves in a large bowl. Cover and refrigerate overnight to marinate.

Preheat the oven to 350°F. Arrange the chicken in a single layer in 1 or 2 large, shallow baking pans. Evenly spoon with the marinade. Sprinkle the chicken pieces with the brown sugar, and pour the white wine around them.

Bake for 45 minutes, or until the chicken is done, basting frequently with pan juices.

Transfer the chicken, prunes, olives and capers to a serving platter using a slotted spoon. Drizzle with few spoonfuls of pan juices and sprinkle generously with the parsley. Pass the remaining pan juices in a sauceboat.

Alternatively, serve at room temperature. Cool in the cooking juices before transferring to a serving platter if warm. If the chicken has been covered and refrigerated, allow it to return to room temperature before serving. Spoon some of the reserved juice over chicken.

Chicken with Mushroom Sauce

Serves 4

Mushroom Sauce

3 tablespoons butter
8 ounces fresh mushrooms, sliced
3 tablespoons flour
1½ cups chicken broth
1 tablespoon minced fresh chives
1 tablespoon minced fresh parsley leaves
1 teaspoon Dijon mustard
¼ teaspoon salt
Freshly ground black pepper to taste
½ cup sour cream

Chicken

1 tablespoon vegetable oil
4 boneless, skinless chicken breast halves
4 slices ham (optional)
4 slices Monterey Jack cheese
½ red bell pepper, cut into thin strips

To prepare the mushroom sauce, melt the butter in medium saucepan over medium heat. Add the mushrooms; cook until tender. Remove with a slotted spoon to a plate. Stir the flour into the pan and cook until bubbly. Slowly whisk in the broth. Add the mushrooms, chives, parsley, mustard, salt, and pepper. Cook, stirring constantly, until thickened. Stir in the sour cream and continue cooking until warmed through. Do not boil. Cover and keep warm on very low heat.

To prepare the chicken, heat a large skillet on medium and add the oil. Sauté the chicken about 8 minutes, turning occasionally, until chicken is browned and cooked through. Reduce the heat to low. Place a slice of ham on each piece of chicken, if desired. Top the ham or the chicken with the cheese. Cover and cook 1 to 2 minutes, or just until the cheese melts. Spoon the mushroom sauce over the chicken and top with the red pepper strips. For a variation, serve the chicken on toasted English muffins.

Fat-free half & half or sour cream perform the same as their heavier cousins. In cooking with them, there is no difference in taste or texture.

~

The frying pan built in 1950 for use at the Delmarva Chicken Festival is 10 feet in diameter, and holds 800 chicken quarters and 180 gallons of oil.

Barratt's Chapel,
in Sussex County, Delaware,
is known as "The Cradle
of Methodism in America."
Built on land deeded by
Col. Philip Barratt in August
1780, it is the oldest surviving
church built by and for
Methodists in the U.S.

Curried Chicken Curl Ups

Serves 6

Chicken

6 boneless, skinless chicken breasts
¼ cup plus 2 tablespoons butter, divided
1 small apple, chopped
¼ cup chopped onion
½ cup raisins or currants
½ cup slivered almonds
¼ teaspoon ground ginger
2 teaspoons curry powder
½ teaspoon cinnamon
½ teaspoon ground cloves

Sauce

4 tablespoons butter
3 tablespoons flour
¼ cup white wine
2 cups milk
1½ teaspoons curry powder
½ teaspoon ground cloves

Spray a 9 x 13-inch baking dish with nonstick cooking oil. Preheat the oven to 350°F. Heat a large skillet on medium-high and melt ¼ cup of the butter. Sauté the apples and onions 3 to 5 minutes, or until the onions are translucent. Remove from the heat and stir in the raisins, almonds, ginger, curry, ¼ teaspoon of the cinnamon, and ¼ teaspoon of the cloves.

Pound each chicken breast to ¼ inch thick. Place a heaping tablespoon-or more for larger breasts-in the center of each breast. Roll up the breasts and place in the baking dish, seam-side down.

Melt the remaining 2 tablespoons of butter in a small bowl and stir in the remaining ¼ teaspoons of cinnamon and cloves. Baste the chicken generously and sprinkle any remaining stuffing on top. Cover with foil and bake for 1 hour.

The chicken can be prepared ahead up to this point and frozen until ready to complete.

To prepare the sauce, melt the butter in a medium pan over medium heat. Whisk in the flour and let it cook slightly. Gradually add the white wine and milk, whisking constantly. Stir in the curry and cloves, and cook another 5 minutes, stirring frequently.

Curried Chicken Curl Ups, continued

Remove the chicken from the oven and pour with the sauce. (If frozen, defrost the curl-ups first and then cover with the sauce.) Return to the oven and cook another 15 to 30 minutes. Serve hot over rice.

♪ *A great dish for entertaining, as it can be made ahead of time. For a sweeter flavor, add ⅓ cup of chutney to the sauce.*

Chicken in Lemon Sauce

Serves 8

¼ cup butter
4 whole skinless, boneless chicken breasts, cut in half
2 tablespoons dry white wine
½ teaspoon grated lemon zest
2 tablespoons freshly squeezed lemon juice
¼ teaspoon salt
⅛ teaspoon white pepper
1 cup heavy cream
⅓ cup freshly grated Parmesan cheese
1 cup sliced fresh mushrooms
Red grapes, for garnish

Melt the butter in large skillet over medium heat. Sauté the chicken about 10 minutes, turning occasionally, or until the chicken is browned and tender. Place the chicken in an ovenproof serving dish and preheat the broiler. Discard the butter from the skillet. Return the heat to medium-high and add the wine, lemon zest, and lemon juice to deglaze the skillet. Cook, scraping up any browned bits with a wooden spoon. Reduce the heat to medium and stir in the salt and white pepper. Gradually pour in the cream, stirring constantly until heated through; do not boil. Pour the cream sauce over the chicken; sprinkle with the cheese and mushrooms. Broil the chicken about 6 inches from the heat until lightly browned. Garnish with the grapes.

In marinades or sauces, you can substitute broth or fruit juice for wine in some recipes. But be aware that doing so may lessen the full-bodied flavor of a dish.

The Lewes Historical Complex is a collection of restored buildings, including the Burton-Ingram House (c. 1789), Hiram Burton House (c. 1780), a turn-of-the-century doctor's office, a Swedish-style Plank House furnished as a settler's cabin, a blacksmith's shop, gift shop, and Thompson country store (c. 1800). Tours are available by appointment.

Béarnaise Chicken

Serves 8

1 pound ground sausage with sage
¾ cup all-purpose flour
1 teaspoon chopped fresh thyme leaves
1 teaspoon salt
1 teaspoon freshly ground black pepper
8 skinless, boneless chicken breast halves
⅓ cup vegetable oil
2 envelopes béarnaise sauce
1 (14 ounce) can artichoke hearts, drained and halved
⅓ cup pecans, plus more for garnish
Fresh thyme sprigs or sage leaves, for garnish

Preheat the oven to 350°F. Lightly grease an 11 x 17-inch baking dish. Brown the sausage in large skillet over medium-high heat, stirring until it crumbles. Drain on paper towels and discard the drippings from the skillet. Combine the flour, thyme, salt, and pepper. Dredge the chicken in the flour mixture. Return the skillet to the stovetop and heat the oil over medium-high heat. Add the chicken to the skillet and brown on both sides. Drain the chicken and set aside.

Prepare béarnaise sauce according to package directions using the reduced-calorie instructions. Spread the sausage in the baking dish. Layer with the chicken breasts, artichoke halves, béarnaise sauce, and chopped pecans. Bake for 40 to 45 minutes, or until the chicken is no longer pink inside. Garnish with additional pecans and fresh sprigs of thyme.

♪ *Wild rice is a perfect side dish.*

Country Style Chicken Kiev

Serves 4

½ cup fine bread crumbs

2 tablespoons freshly grated Parmesan Cheese

1 teaspoon chopped fresh oregano

1 teaspoon chopped fresh basil

½ teaspoon garlic salt

¼ teaspoon salt

4 chicken breast halves

⅔ cup butter, melted

¼ cup white wine

¼ cup chopped green onion

¼ cup chopped fresh parsley leaves

Preheat the oven to 375°F. Combine the bread crumbs, Parmesan, oregano, basil, garlic salt, and salt in a shallow bowl. Dip the chicken in the butter, then in the bread crumb mixture. (Reserve any extra butter.) Place the prepared chicken in a baking dish. Bake 50 to 60 minutes. Combine the remaining butter with the wine, green onions, and parsley. When the chicken is golden, pour the butter sauce over chicken and continue baking 3 to 5 minutes.

Today about 500 descendants of the original Nanticoke Indians reside in Delaware. They celebrate their heritage each September with the Nanticoke Indian Pow Wow, held in Millsboro.

The Amstel House
reflects the style and
refinement of New Castle's
early prosperity. Graced
with original woodworking,
architectural details and
finely carved cornices, it is a
fine example of early Georgian
architecture. Built in the
1730s by Dr. John Finney,
the house is linked with
prominent historical families.
George Washington attended
a wedding reception here,
signers of the Declaration of
Independence stopped in to meet
with friends, and it was once a
governor's home. The Amstel
House interprets 18th and
19th century life in
New Castle.

Grilled Chicken in Two Directions

Serves 4

Spicy Peach Glaze

2 cups peach preserves or jam
1 tablespoon finely chopped garlic
2 tablespoons soy sauce
1 tablespoon Dijon mustard
1 small jalapeño, finely chopped
4 ripe peaches, cut in half and pitted

Avocado Corn Salsa

1 ear corn, roasted
1 avocado, diced
¼ cup minced red onion
¼ cup minced red bell pepper
½ teaspoon minced garlic
2 dashes hot pepper sauce
1 teaspoon ground cumin
¼ teaspoon chile powder
3 tablespoons chopped fresh cilantro leaves
1 tablespoon freshly squeezed lime juice

Grilled Chicken

4 boneless chicken breasts
Olive oil as needed
Salt and freshly ground black pepper to taste
1 cup lemon juice

If preparing the Spicy Peach Glaze, combine the preserves, garlic, soy, mustard, and jalapeño. Reserve ½ cup of the mixture. (Use the remaining glaze to brush both sides of the chicken during the last 5 minutes of cooking.) Place the peach halves, cut-side down on the grill and cook for 2 minutes. Turn over and brush with the reserved ½ cup of peach glaze. Grill an additional 3 to 4 minutes, or until the peaches are soft.

If preparing the Avocado Corn Salsa, cut the kernels off the cob. Combine all the ingredients and store in an airtight container in the refrigerator until ready to use. (If preferred, roast the ear of corn on the grill while cooking the chicken and add to the salsa at the last minute.)

Grilled Chicken in Two Directions, continued

Prepare the grill to a high heat. Brush the chicken with the olive oil and season with salt and pepper. Brush with the lemon juice. Grill 10 to 15 minutes total, turning 3 times. If serving with the glaze, brush the chicken during the last 5 minutes of grilling. Serve the chicken with either the Spicy Peach Glaze or the Avocado Corn Salsa.

♪ *This recipe offers two different techniques for grilled chicken, both delicious.*

There's rosemary, that's for remembrance...
~ Hamlet, IV, v, 174

Roast Turkey Breast with Garlic and Rosemary
Serves 4 to 6

1 skinless turkey breast, bone in
2 cloves garlic, slivered
Several tiny sprigs fresh rosemary or ½ teaspoon dried
3 tablespoons honey
1 tablespoon Dijon mustard
1 tablespoon olive oil
1 tablespoon freshly squeezed lemon juice
½ teaspoon freshly ground black pepper
Salt to taste

Preheat the oven to 350°F.

Make small slits in the top of the turkey breast and insert the garlic slivers and fresh rosemary needles. (If using dried rosemary, combine it with the honey mixture.) Combine the honey, mustard, oil, lemon juice, and pepper. Brush over the breast. Sprinkle with salt. Place the turkey in a baking dish, meaty-side up. Roast for 60 minutes, or until the juices run clear. Baste every 10 minutes.

The Union fortress located on Pea Patch Island in the Delaware River dates back to 1859. Originally built to protect the ports of Wilmington and Philadelphia, it served as a prison for Confederate prisoners during the Civil War. In 1951 it became one of Delaware's first state parks, and was placed on the National Register of Historic Places twenty years later.

Rock Cornish Game Hens with Pine Nut Stuffing

Serves 4

8 tablespoons melted butter, plus additional for brushing
2 medium onions, finely chopped
2 cups cooked rice
2 teaspoons chopped fresh tarragon leaves
1½ teaspoons salt
½ teaspoon freshly ground black pepper
4 tablespoons cognac
¼ cup pine nuts
4 Cornish game hens, rinsed and patted dry

Preheat the oven to 350°F. Melt the butter in a large sauté pan and cook the onion until transparent. Add the rice, tarragon, salt, pepper, cognac, and nuts; mix well. Stuff the hens with the mixture and cover the openings with aluminum foil. Brush the hens well with butter and place in a large roasting pan. Bake for 30 to 45 minutes, or until brown and tender. Baste occasionally with the pan juices.

Teriyaki Flank Steak

Serves 2 to 3

Marinade

1 cup pineapple juice
½ cup oil
2 cloves garlic
3 ounces soy sauce
½ cup packed dark brown sugar

1 (1 pound) beef flank steak

Combine the marinade ingredients with an electric mixer to emulsify. Place the flank steak in a 13 x 9-inch pan and pour the marinade over the steak. Marinate for at least 8 hours in the refrigerator.

Prepare the grill. Grill the steak to the desired degree of doneness, turning and basting frequently. Cut flank steak across the grain at a slight angle into thin slices.

♪ *This recipe has its origins in Okinawa and also works well for marinating beef for shish kebobs.*

Beef Tenderloin with Mushroom Stuffing

Serves 6 to 8

¼ cup butter

1 medium onion, chopped

½ cup diced celery

6 ounces fresh mushrooms, preferably a combination of cremini and portobellos

2 cups soft bread crumbs, preferably day-old baguette

1 teaspoon sea salt

1 teaspoon freshly ground black pepper

1 teaspoon snipped fresh basil leaves

½ teaspoon snipped fresh parsley leaves

3 to 4 pounds beef tenderloin

4 slices of bacon, cut in half

Preheat the oven to 350°F.

Melt the butter in a large sauté pan over medium heat. Sauté the onions, celery, and mushrooms until soft. Combine the bread crumbs with the salt, pepper, basil, and parsley in a medium bowl. Stir in the sautéed vegetables.

Slice the tenderloin lengthwise, being careful not to cut all the way through. (The tenderloin should open like a book.) Mound the stuffing mixture the length of the tenderloin and close the tenderloin. Fasten with toothpicks to secure. Place the loin in a roasting pan and lay the bacon slices crosswise across the top of the meat. Bake, uncovered, for 45 minutes for medium-rare or 1 hour for medium. Remove from the oven and let rest 5 minutes. Place on a warm serving platter, pour with the cooking juices, and slice to serve.

Visitors take a ferry ride to Pea Patch Island, then a jitney to the granite and brick fortress. There are living history tours and interactive programs, including the loading and firing of a giant 8-inch Rodman seacoast cannon, infantry drills, and evening ghost tours. The view from the ramparts is fascinating, as sea-going vessels from around the world pass within a few hundred feet of the island.

Pea Patch Island also offers many natural treasures. The island is the summer home to nine different species of herons, egrets and ibis. The remote marshes provide an outstanding habitat, making Pea Patch Island the largest Atlantic Coast nesting ground north of Florida for wading birds.

A hiking trail and an observation tower provide an opportunity to see these beautiful birds flying to and from their rookery.

Stuffed Beef Tenderloin
Serves 10 to 12

¼ cup butter
1 pound fresh mushrooms, sliced, plus additional for garnish
1 cup chipped scallions, green and white parts, chopped
¼ cup chopped fresh parsley leaves
1 (6 to 7 pound) beef tenderloin, butterflied
½ teaspoon seasoned salt
¼ teaspoon lemon pepper
4 ounces blue cheese, crumbled
1 (8 ounce) bottle red wine vinegar and oil dressing
Black peppercorns, crushed
Salt to taste
Watercress, for garnish

Heat a large skillet on medium-high and add the butter. Sauté the mushrooms and scallions until tender. Remove from the skillet with a slotted spoon and mix with the parsley. Sprinkle the interior of the loin with the seasoned salt and lemon pepper, spoon with the mushroom mixture, and then top with the cheese. Fold the two sides of the loin together and tie with butcher's twine at 2-inch intervals. Set the tenderloin in a baking dish or in a large zipperlock bag. Pour the dressing over the tenderloin. Cover and refrigerate at least 8 hours, basting occasionally.

Prepare a grill to a medium-hot fire. Remove from the marinade and press the crushed peppercorns onto each side of the tenderloin. Season with salt. Grill for 35 minutes for rare, 45 minutes for medium. Alternatively, bake at 350°F. for 40 minutes. Garnish with watercress and mushrooms.

Peppercorn Beef Tenderloin

Serves 8

½ cup soy sauce, divided
2 teaspoons freshly ground pink peppercorns
2 teaspoons freshly ground green peppercorns
2 teaspoons freshly ground black peppercorns
2 teaspoons ground ginger
1½ teaspoons ground cardamom
8 cloves garlic, minced
1 (4 pound) beef tenderloin, trimmed of fat

Combine 2 tablespoons of the soy sauce with the pink pepper-corns, green peppercorns, black peppercorns, ginger, cardamom, and garlic. Stir well and rub over the tenderloin. Place the tender-loin in a large, plastic zipperlock bag, and pour in the remaining soy sauce. Seal the bag and marinate in the refrigerator for 8 hours, turning the bag occasionally.

Preheat the oven to 425°F. Remove the tenderloin from the bag, reserving the marinade, and pat dry. Place the tenderloin on a roasting rack coated with cooking spray; place the rack in a roasting pan.

Bake at 425°F for 45 minutes, or until a meat thermometer registers 140°F. for rare or 160°F. for medium, basting tenderloin frequently with the reserved marinade.

Place the tenderloin on a large serving platter and let stand 10 minutes before slicing.

The Biggs Museum, in Dover, houses fourteen galleries of American fine and decorative arts assembled over the past sixty years by the founder, Sewell C. Biggs. Paintings that span two centuries provide a survey of major styles of American art, from colonial portraiture to impressionism. Artists of note include members of the Peale family, Gilbert Stuart, Thomas Cole, Albert Bierstadt, and Childe Hassam. A special feature is the focus on artists from the region, such as Delaware illustrator Frank E. Schoonover. The exhibition of furniture and silver highlights the work of Delaware Valley craftsmen. Sculpture, needle-work, drawings, and ceramics complement the exceptional display of American art.

Dover Air Force Base is home to the gigantic C-5 cargo planes, whose 223-foot wingspan and 65-foot height makes them visible to beachgoers coming and going on Route 1. Each of these planes can carry 270,000 pounds of cargo, including such bulky items as the Army's 74-ton mobile scissors bridge.

Walnut and Blue Cheese Butter on Steaks

Serves 6

6 ounces crumbled blue cheese

½ stick butter, room temperature

2 tablespoons chopped fresh parsley leaves

1 tablespoon plus 1 teaspoon finely chopped dried rosemary, divided

¼ cup chopped walnuts, toasted

1½ teaspoons salt, plus more to taste

1½ teaspoons ground black pepper, plus more to taste

6 large cloves garlic, peeled

2 (1½ to 1¾ pound) top sirloin steaks, about 1 inch thick

Combine the blue cheese, butter, parsley and ¾ teaspoon of the rosemary in medium bowl. Stir to blend well. Stir in the walnuts, and season with salt and pepper to taste. Cover and refrigerate if not using immediately. (Allow the butter to return to room temperature before serving.)

Combine the remaining 1 tablespoon plus ¼ teaspoon of the rosemary with the garlic, 1½ teaspoons of the salt, and 1½ tea-spoons of the pepper in a food processor. Blend until the mixture resembles a coarse paste. Place the steaks in a large baking dish and rub each side of the steaks with 2 teaspoons of the garlic mixture. Cover and refrigerate for at least 2 hours before grilling.

Prepare the grill to a medium-high heat. Grill the steaks until the desired degree of doneness and let stand 5 minutes before slicing. Slice each steak into 3 equal portions and top each portion with a spoonful of blue cheese butter. Serve any of the extra butter with French bread or potatoes.

Marinated Flank Steak

Serves 3 to 4

Marinade

¼ cup sesame seeds, toasted
¼ cup chopped scallions, green and white parts
3 tablespoons soy sauce
2 tablespoons sesame oil
1 tablespoon cider vinegar
1 tablespoon packed dark brown sugar
1 tablespoon peeled and minced fresh ginger
1 tablespoon minced garlic
1 teaspoon dry mustard
1 teaspoon Worcestershire sauce

1½ pounds flank steak

Crush the sesame seeds with mortar and pestle. Combine all the marinade ingredients in a large glass dish or a plastic zipperlock bag. Add the flank steak and refrigerate at least 4 hours or overnight. Prepare the grill to a high heat. Grill 4 inches above hot coals for 5 minutes on each side, basting frequently. Slice thinly on the diagonal and serve hot.

To garnish a plate with herbs, apply a light coating of oil or melted butter to the plate rim with a pastry brush. Sprinkle chopped herbs, nuts, or spices (consistent with the appearance and flavor of the food) over the rim, and tilt the plate to let excess garnish fall away. The entire plate rim may be garnished, or just the outer edge.

*"French-fried potatoes"
didn't originate in France.
The name refers to a method
of preparing certain foods
known as "Frenching." Meats
and vegetables, notably beans,
are "Frenched" ~ cut into
narrow strips ~ before cooking.
So it was only logical that these
popular strips of potatoes
became known as
French fries.*

Grilled Flank Steak

Serves 3 to 4

Steak

1½ pounds flank steak, trimmed of fat and membrane
1 tablespoon olive oil
Freshly ground black pepper

Sauce

3 cloves garlic
Pinch of coarse sea salt
3 anchovies
4 tablespoons olive oil
1½ tablespoons chopped fresh Italian parsley leaves

Season the steak with the pepper and then rub in the olive oil. Marinate in the refrigerator for 2 hours.

To prepare the sauce, put the garlic and a pinch of salt in the mortar, and reduce to a pulp. Add the anchovies and continue to mash. Add the olive oil and parsley, and mix well.

Prepare the grill to a high heat. Grill the steak, covered, for 3 or 4 minutes per side until medium rare. Slice thinly across the grain and slide carefully onto a warm serving platter. Spoon the sauce down the center of the meat and serve immediately.

♪ *This is a great excuse to use that forgotten Armetale platter. It will keep the meat hot.*

Cranberry Pot Roast

Serves 6 to 8

2 tablespoons flour

1 teaspoon salt

1 teaspoon onion salt

¼ teaspoon freshly ground black pepper

2 tablespoons butter

3 to 4 pound roast

4 whole cloves

1 teaspoon cinnamon

½ cup plus 2 tablespoons water, divided

1 (16 ounce) can whole cranberry sauce

1 tablespoon vinegar

Combine the flour, salt, onion salt, and pepper. Rub the mixture into the roast. Melt the butter in a Dutch oven over medium heat and brown the meat on all sides. Remove the pan from the heat. Add the cloves, cinnamon, and ½ cup of the water. Cover tightly and simmer about 2½ hours, or until tender, adding more water if needed. Spoon off any fat. Combine the cranberry sauce, vinegar, and the remaining 2 tablespoons of water; add to the meat. Cover and cook 10 to 15 minutes longer. Remove the roast to a warm serving platter and pour the pan juices into a gravy boat to pass with the meat.

An important link in the Atlantic Flyway from Canada to the Gulf of Mexico, the Bombay Hook National Wildlife Refuge near Smyrna shelters more than 250 species of birds, 33 species of mammals, and 37 species of amphibians and reptiles. For visitors, getting around is easy thanks to a 12-mile, round-trip auto tour and several nature trails for walking, three of which have 30-foot observation towers.

*Georgetown, Delaware,
is the location for a unique
political tradition known as
Return Day. Following an
election, winners and losers
ride together in a carriage
parade to the historic circle
in Georgetown, for the
official reading of the election
results by the Town Crier.
Then both winner and loser
"bury the hatchet" in a special
ceremony, followed by live
music, political speeches, and
an old-fashioned ox roast.*

Beef Brisket

Serves 6

Brisket

3 to 4 pounds beef brisket
Meat tenderizer (optional)

Sauce

1 (12 ounce) bottle chili sauce
1 tablespoon caraway seed
1 tablespoon chili powder
½ cup red wine vinegar or cider vinegar
2 green onions, chopped
2 stalks celery, chopped
¼ cup packed dark brown sugar
¼ teaspoon liquid smoke

Preheat the oven to 275°F. Sprinkle both sides of brisket with the tenderizer, if desired. Place the meat fat-side up in heavy duty foil and place in a roasting pan or 13 x 9 baking dish. Combine the sauce ingredients together and pour over the meat. Cover tightly with foil and roast for 5 hours. Remove from the oven, let rest 15 minutes, and slice.

♪ *This dish can be served with roasted red potatoes or on crusty rolls to an afternoon crowd. It is not too hot or spicy for most people and is a simple dish to make.*

Burgundy Fondue
Serves 4

10 ounces Burgundy wine

10 ounces beef stock

1 medium onion, chopped

Chopped fresh parsley

1 teaspoon dried marjoram

1 teaspoon garlic salt

2 pounds raw beef, fish, shrimp, mushrooms, and or other vegetables, cubed

Dipping sauces, such as horseradish sauce, sour cream, hot mustard, barbecue sauce, etc.

Combine the wine, stock, onion, parsley, marjoram, and garlic salt in a stock pot and bring to a boil. Cover, remove from heat, and let stand for 2 hours. Strain and discard the onion and parsley. Pour the liquid into a fondue pot to come at least 2 inches up the sides. Set the pot over the flame until the liquid is very hot. Place the dipping sauces in small serving bowls and place around the fondue pot. Provide each participant with a fondue fork. Dip individual pieces of meat, fish, or vegetables in the hot liquid until cooked. Dip into the preferred sauce and enjoy.

♪ *This is great for a relaxed get–together or party.*

When recipes call for only a little wine, small bottles ~ called splits ~ are the best to buy.

The state's Coastal Heritage Greenway consists of a corridor of open space running along 90 miles of coastline, spanning the area between Fox Point State Park and the Delaware state line at Fenwick Island.

Veal Piccata
Serves 4

1½ tablespoons flour
Paprika
Salt and freshly ground black pepper to taste
½ stick butter
1 pound veal scaloppine
¼ cup white wine
½ cup chicken stock
2 tablespoons freshly squeezed lemon juice
3 tablespoons heavy cream
1 tablespoon capers

Combine the flour, paprika, salt, and pepper. Heat a large skillet on medium-high and melt the butter. Dredge the veal in the flour mixture and sauté in batches in the butter until just browned on both sides. (Reserve the flour and do not overcook the veal.) Place the cooked veal on a plate and set aside. When all the veal has been browned, sprinkle the remaining flour mixture in the skillet and cook, stirring until brown. Deglaze the pan with the wine, scraping up the browned bits to add flavor. Simmer until almost completely reduced, and then add the chicken stock. Return the veal to the pan.

Add the veal and any juices to the sauce and simmer, covered, for 5 to 10 minutes. Remove the veal to a serving platter and keep warm. To finish the sauce, stir in the lemon juice, heavy cream, and capers. Simmer and stir for 1 to 2 minutes. Pour over the veal and serve immediately.

Marinade for Pork Chops or Chicken
Marinade for 4 servings of meat

½ cup soy sauce
¼ cup white sugar
2 tablespoons vinegar
Garlic powder to taste

Combine all the ingredients in a small bowl. Use to marinate pork chops or chicken breasts for several hours before cooking. Baste frequently with the marinade while baking or grilling the meat.

Crock Pot Pork Chops and Sauerkraut

Serves 4

1 (28 ounce) can or bag sauerkraut, with juice
1 tablespoon packed dark brown sugar
1 onion, chopped
1 to 2 tablespoons olive oil, for sautéing
4 thick-cut pork chops
Garlic powder to taste
Salt and freshly ground black pepper to taste

Combine the sauerkraut, brown sugar, and onion in a small bowl. Heat a large skillet on medium-high and add the olive oil. Brown the pork chops in the olive oil and season with the garlic powder, salt, and pepper to taste. Layer the browned chops and the sauerkraut mixture in crock pot. Cook for 6 hours on high.

♪ *This dish will make anyone a sauerkraut convert.*

An idealist is one who, on noticing that a rose smells better than a cabbage, concludes that it will also make better soup.

~ H.L. Mencken

Creole Pork Chops

Serves 6 to 8

2 tablespoons shortening
6 to 8 pork chops, cut 1 inch thick
1 teaspoon Tabasco sauce
1 teaspoon Worcestershire sauce
¼ teaspoon freshly ground black pepper
½ cup ketchup
½ cup water
2 tablespoons packed dark brown sugar
1 teaspoon salt

Heat a large sauté pan on medium-high. Melt the shortening and brown the chops on both sides. Combine the Tabasco, Worcestershire, pepper, ketchup, water, brown sugar, and salt in a small bowl. Pour the mixture over the chops, cover, and simmer for 1 to 1½ hours.

*Instead of scrubbing
a pan that has a burnt on
gooey mess, fill it with
hot water and drop in a
dryer sheet (such as Bounce).
Let it soak for an hour or so,
and the mess will
wipe right off.*

Pork in Red Wine

Serves 6

4 pounds pork loin
Salt and freshly ground black pepper to taste
Powdered sage to taste
Garlic powder to taste
Nutmeg to taste
2 tablespoons oil
2 cups dry red wine
¼ cup chopped fresh parsley leaves
1 bay leaf
1 (10½ ounce) can consommé or beef broth, or more if needed
½ cup chopped onion
4 tablespoons cornstarch
6 tablespoons water

Preheat the oven to 350°F.

Rub the pork loin with the salt, pepper, sage, garlic powder, and nutmeg. Heat a large roasting pan on high and add the oil. Brown the pork loin on all sides. Remove the pork loin to a separate plate. Deglaze the pan with the wine, scraping up the browned bits for added flavor. Add the parsley, bay leaf, consommé, and onion. Return the pork loin to the pan, turning to coat with the mixture. Bake, uncovered, about 2 hours, turning occasionally, until the pork registers 150°F. on a meat thermometer.

Remove the pork to a warm serving platter and let rest while finishing the sauce. Set the roasting pan and juices on the stovetop over high heat. Combine the cornstarch with the water in a small bowl. Add to the pan to thicken the sauce, stirring well to incorporate. For more sauce, add another can of consommé. Slice the pork loin and serve with the warm sauce.

Sautéed Pork Tenderloin with Vermouth Sauce

Serves 4 to 6

1 tablespoon butter
1 tablespoon oil
2 pork tenderloins (about ¾ pound each)
1 teaspoon dried rosemary, crumbled
1 teaspoon dried thyme
⅛ teaspoon salt
½ teaspoon freshly ground black pepper
2 cups dry vermouth
1 cup half-and-half

Preheat the oven to 100°F. Heat a large skillet on high and add the butter and oil. When hot, add the tenderloins and sear until brown on all sides. Add the rosemary, thyme, salt, and pepper. Deglaze with the vermouth, scraping the bottom of the pan with any browned bits. Cover, reduce the heat to medium-low, and simmer for 30 minutes, or until a meat thermometer registers 150°F. (The meat will be slightly pink in the middle.) Remove the tenderloins and keep warm in the oven, reserving the sauce in the skillet. Bring the sauce to a boil over medium-high heat until reduced by half. Reduce the heat to low, stir in the half-and-half, and heat through; do not boil. Remove the pork from oven and cut into ½-inch slices. Arrange on warm serving plates and spoon about ⅛ cup over each serving.

♪ *Good accompanied with wild rice.*

Use tongs or a flat utensil to turn meat during cooking. A fork will puncture the seared crust, releasing the meat's juices and leaving it dry.

In 1802, Eleuthére Irenée du Pont established a gunpowder mill near Wilmington that laid the foundation for Delaware's huge chemical industry. Delaware's manufactured products now also include textiles, paper, medical supplies, vulcanized fiber, metal products, machinery, machine tools, and automobiles.

Pork Tenderloin Aux Duxelles

Serves 4

Pork

1 pound pork tenderloin
Salt and freshly ground black pepper to taste
1 to 1½ tablespoons butter
3 to 4 strips bacon

Stuffing

2 tablespoons butter
1 medium onion, finely chopped
¼ teaspoon dried thyme
¼ teaspoon dried sage
3 ounces mushrooms, finely chopped
1 egg
2 tablespoons cream
4 ounces fresh bread crumbs
4 tablespoons chopped fresh parsley leaves
Grated zest of 1 lemon
2 teaspoons freshly squeezed lemon juice
Salt and freshly ground black pepper

Gravy

1 tablespoon brown flour
1 cup dry white wine or dry cider
Salt and freshly ground black pepper to taste

To prepare the pork, preheat the oven to 350°F. Grease a roasting pan with the butter. Leave the fat on the tenderloin to help keep it moist, but remove the silver skin for a prettier presentation. With a sharp knife, split the tenderloin in half lengthwise. Cover with a piece of wax paper or plastic wrap and pound the halves to flatten and widen them slightly. Season with salt and pepper.

To prepare the stuffing, heat a large saucepan on medium and add the butter. Sauté the onions, thyme, and sage and herbs for about 10 minutes. Add the mushrooms and increase the heat to medium-high. Cook 3 to 4 minutes, or until the juices from the mushrooms have almost evaporated. Beat the egg with the cream in a large bowl. Stir in the bread crumbs, parsley, lemon zest, and lemon juice with a fork. Stir in the mushroom mixture and season to taste.

Pork Tenderloin Aux Duxelles, continued

Spoon the stuffing onto one of the tenderloin halves, patting it down slightly, and then top with the other tenderloin half. Smear with some butter and season with pepper. Cover the top of the tenderloin with the bacon and tie with string at 2 inch intervals to stabilize. Transfer the stuffed tenderloin to the roasting pan. Bake for 1 hour, and then place on a warmed serving platter and let rest 5 minutes before slicing. Reserve the roasting pan and juices to make the gravy.

Set the roasting pan over high heat on the stovetop and stir the flour into the pan juices, cooking to remove any flour taste. Deglaze the pan with the wine, scraping up the browned bits with a wooden spoon for added flavor. Season with salt and pepper, and whisk until smooth. To serve, carve the meat into thick slices and pour some gravy over each slice.

Pork Chops in Frozen Marinade

Serves 4 to 6

4 to 6 thin pork chops

Marinade

2 teaspoons peeled and minced fresh ginger

2 teaspoons dry mustard

2 teaspoons salt

1 teaspoon freshly ground black pepper

2 cloves garlic, minced

2 tablespoons Worcestershire sauce

½ cup freshly squeezed lemon juice

½ cup cooking oil

¼ cup honey

Place the pork chops in a gallon-size, plastic zipperlock bag. Combine the marinade ingredients in small bowl and pour the marinade over the chops. Seal the bag and place in a flat casserole dish in the freezer to keep the packages flat. (Once frozen, you can remove the casserole dish.) The morning you want to serve the chops, remove the bag from the freezer and allow to defrost on a plate in the refrigerator. Prepare the grill to a medium heat. Remove the chops from the marinade and grill until the pork is crispy around the edges.

Delaware grows a great variety of fruits and vegetables, and is a U.S. pioneer in the food-canning industry. Corn, soybeans, potatoes, and hay are also important crops. Sussex County, Delaware is the nation's leading poultry producer. Fishing and dairy products are also important industries.

*Odessa possesses
one of the finest collections
of late 18th- and early
19th-century architecture
in the middle Atlantic region.
The center of town is on the
National Register of Historic
Places, and the entire town has
been zoned as historic.*

Ginger and Honey Pork Tenderloin

Serves 4 to 6

2 (¾ pound) pork tenderloins, trimmed of fat and silver skin

Marinade

¼ **cup honey**
¼ **cup soy sauce**
2 tablespoons packed dark brown sugar
2 tablespoons peeled and minced fresh ginger
2 tablespoons minced garlic
1 tablespoon ketchup
¼ **teaspoon onion powder**
¼ **teaspoon cayenne pepper**

Pat the pork dry and place in shallow dish or large plastic zipperlock bag. Whisk together all the marinade ingredients and pour over the pork. Turn the pork to coat well. Cover and chill at least 8 hours and up to 1 day, turning once or twice.

Preheat the oven to 425°F. or prepare the grill. To bake, place the tenderloins in a baking dish along with the marinade. Bake about 35 minutes, or until a meat thermometer registers 150°F. (The meat will be slightly pink.) To grill, remove the pork from the marinade and reserve the marinade. Place the tenderloin on a lightly oiled rack set 5 to 6 inches over glowing coals. Grill the pork, basting with the reserved marinade and turning every 3 minutes, 10 minutes total. Discard the marinade. Continue to cook the pork, turning every 3 minutes until a thermometer inserted 2 inches into the center registers 150°F., about 10 minutes more. Let stand 5 minutes before thinly slicing.

Bourbon Barbequed Ribs
Serves 4 to 6

4 pounds baby back ribs

Sauce

½ **cup light molasses**
½ **cup ketchup**
⅓ **cup orange juice**
2 **tablespoons cooking oil**
1 **tablespoon vinegar**
1 **tablespoon steak sauce**
½ **teaspoon prepared mustard**
½ **teaspoon Worcestershire sauce**
¼ **teaspoon garlic**
¼ **teaspoon salt**
¼ **teaspoon pepper**
¼ **teaspoon Tabasco sauce**
⅛ **teaspoon ground cloves**
¼ **cup bourbon**

Bring a large pot of water to a boil and add the ribs. Reduce the heat and simmer for 40 to 50 minutes. While the ribs are cooking, combine all the sauce ingredients in a large saucepan. Bring to a boil, reduce the heat, and simmer for 20 minutes. Prepare the grill. Remove the ribs from the water and add to the sauce. Grill the ribs, turning and basting every 15 minutes. Cut the ribs apart for easier serving.

♪ *For extra-saucy ribs, double or triple the sauce recipe.*

Augustine Beach was named for Augustine Hermann, a Bohemian adventurer who mapped the Delmarva Peninsula and surrounding areas in the mid-1600s.

Holy Trinity (Old Swedes) Church in Wilmington, is the nation's oldest church building still standing as originally built, and in regular use for worship. Dedicated on Holy Trinity Sunday, July 4, 1699, Old Swedes was designated a Registered National Historic Landmark in 1963, in recognition of its unique role for worship by numerous communities of immigrants:

~ the Swedes at Fort Christina and the colony of New Sweden

~ the Dutch in the area centered at New Amstel (now New Castle, Delaware)

~ the English in New Castle County of the colony of Pennsylvania

~ and finally Americans from many nations in the state of Delaware.

An original black walnut pulpit still stands in its original location.

Marinated Pork Tenderloin

Serves 4 to 6

Marinade

⅓ cup sherry
½ cup oil
⅓ cup soy sauce
½ teaspoon ground ginger
½ teaspoon garlic powder

1 to 2 pounds pork tenderloin

Combine all the marinade ingredients in a medium bowl. Place the pork in a plastic zipperlock bag and add the marinade. Refrigerate overnight, turning periodically. Prepare the grill. Remove the pork from the bag, reserving the marinade, and pat dry. Grill for 25 to 30 minutes, turning frequently and basting with the marinade, until a meat thermometer registers 150°F. (The pork will be slightly pink inside.) Remove from the grill and let rest 5 minutes before slicing.

Baked Ham

Serves 20 to 30

1 (15 pound) bone-in smoked ham
1½ cups orange marmalade
1 cup Dijon mustard
1½ cups firmly packed light brown sugar
1 rounded tablespoon whole cloves

Preheat the oven to 300°F. Trim the tough outer skin and excess fat from the ham. Place the ham in a large roasting pan and making cross-hatch incisions all over with a sharp knife. Roast for 2 hours. Remove the ham from oven and increase the heat to 350°F.

To prepare the glaze, combine the orange marmalade, mustard, and brown sugar in a medium bowl. Stud the ham with the cloves, inserting one at the intersection of each crosshatch. Generously brush the entire surface of the ham with the glaze and return to the oven. Cook the ham for 1½ hours more, brushing with the glaze at least 3 times. Remove the ham from the oven and transfer to a cutting board. Let the meat rest about 30 minutes before carving. Serve warm or at room temperature.

Cottage Ham

Serves 4 to 6

1 (2 pound) cottage ham (a smoked, boneless pork shoulder butt)

Marinade

½ cup firmly packed light brown sugar
1 teaspoon dry mustard
½ cup vinegar
½ cup boiling water
½ teaspoon paprika

Preheat the oven to 375°F. Combine the marinade ingredients in a small bowl, stirring well to dissolve. Place the ham in a casserole dish. Pour the marinade over the ham, cover, and bake 35 minutes per pound, basting occasionally.

Turkish Lamb Kebabs

Serves 6 to 8

Marinade

½ cup red wine vinegar
1 tablespoon mixed dried herbs, such as rosemary, thyme, and oregano
5 cloves garlic, crushed
½ cup olive oil
2 tablespoons low-sodium soy sauce
2 tablespoons dry sherry

Kebabs

3 pounds lamb, cubed
Green bell peppers, coarsely chopped
1 (14 ounce) can pineapple chunks
2 white onions, coarsely chopped
Cherry tomatoes
Wooden skewers soaked in water

For a diminutive state, Delaware has numerous nicknames: The First State, Diamond State, Blue Hen State, and Small Wonder.

Combine all the marinade ingredients in a large bowl and whisk thoroughly. Add the lamb to the marinade and refrigerate overnight. Prepare the grill to a medium heat. Soak the wooden skewers in water for 30 minutes to keep them from burning on the grill. Remove the lamb from marinade and pat dry. Slide the cubes onto skewers, alternating with pieces of green pepper, pineapple, onion, and tomato. Grill for 5 to 10 minutes, or to taste. Serve on the skewers over hot rice.

Thomas Jefferson called Delaware a "jewel among the states" because of its strategic location on the Eastern Shore.

Baby Lamb with Lemon Sauce

Serves 6 to 8

3 pounds baby lamb, cubed
Salt and freshly ground black pepper to taste
3 lemons
4 tablespoons olive oil
2 tablespoons butter
1 cup chopped onions
2 ounces prosciutto, finely diced
4 teaspoons all-purpose flour
2 cups dry white wine
3 egg yolks
1 teaspoon grated lemon zest
1 tablespoon finely chopped fresh parsley leaves
1 tablespoon finely chopped fresh marjoram leaves

Season the lamb cubes with salt and pepper. Toss the meat with juice from 1 lemon; mix well to coat thoroughly. Heat the oil and butter in a large sauté pan over medium heat. When the oil and butter is hot, add the lamb, onions, and prosciutto. Cook until the lamb is brown on all sides, about 6 to 8 minutes. Sprinkle the flour over the lamb, stir, and sauté for another minute to cook the flour. Deglaze the pan with the wine, scraping up any browned bits with a wooden spoon, and bring to a simmer. Cover and cook for 30 minutes.

Beat the egg yolks in a small bowl. Whisk in the zest and the juice from the 2 remaining lemons. Spoon some of the hot wine liquid into the egg mixture, whisking to temper the eggs. Slowly stir the egg mixture into the lamb and cook for 2 minutes, continuing to stir so that the eggs won't scramble. Remove from the heat, and stir in the parsley and marjoram. Season with salt and pepper.

Serve over broad egg noodles or rice, and a slice of crusty bread to soak up the sauce.

Herbs & Spices

As a general rule, one teaspoon of dried herbs may be substituted for one tablespoon of the same herb, fresh, and vice versa. The reason a three to one ratio of fresh to dried usually works is that most dried herbs have a more intense, concentrated flavor than their fresh counterparts. However, each herb has its own special character, and some, such as basil, are best used fresh if possible. Of the commonly used cooking herbs, basil, cilantro, parsley and rosemary should be used fresh. Oregano, sage, tarragon and thyme are good fresh or dried. Their flavor is more refined when fresh; dried, they become more robust. If fresh herbs are substituted in a soup or stew, add them toward the end, so that the flavors are not lost by lengthy cooking.

Spice	Taste/Fragrance	Substitutions
Allspice	Similar to natural combination of cloves, cinnamon, and nutmeg.	If you use the same form, (whole for whole, or ground for ground), an equal amount of allspice can be substituted for cinnamon, cloves, or nutmeg, remaining in the same family of tastes.
Basil	From mint family. Mildly aromatic, with warm, sweet, clovelike spiciness. Pungency of dried basil increases with cooking.	
Bay Leaf	Spicy fragrance, similar to bay rum. Pungent flavor.	
Caraway	Bouquet is sweet, warm, slightly peppery; flavor is slightly sharper, reminiscent of aniseed and fennel.	Cumin has stronger, but similar, flavor.
Cardamom	Warm, like eucalyptus, with lemony undertones.	

Herbs & Spices

Use in Cooking	Notes
Particularly popular in European cooking. Use in marinades, mulling spices, patés, and terrines. Enhances dishes made with root vegetables. Also good in cakes, pumpkin or fruit pies, puddings, Middle Eastern meat and rice dishes, Indian curries and pilafs.	Available whole or ground. Ground allspice, even carefully kept, is quite perishable, so if used often, it is better to grind it yourself in a grinder reserved for that purpose.
Goes especially well with tomatoes and pasta dishes; also peas, squash, potatoes, mushrooms, lamb, fish, duck, eggs, cheese, tossed salads, beans & eggplant. Indispensable for many Mediterranean dishes.	Strong enough flavor to stand up to garlic; together they make a classic pesto. Available fresh or dried.
Add bay leaf to water when poaching fish, or to jar for storing & flavoring rice.	Add early in cooking, since it requires much simmering/marinating to flavor food. Always remove before dish is served. Use with parsley & thyme to make bouquet garni. Bay leaves also repel insects ~ use in closets, drawers, or under cabinets.
Good in herb breads, with parsley and/or dill, and sweet biscuits. Add to salads and vegetable dishes, esp. red cabbage, sauerkraut, and potatoes. Enhances pork, duck, goose, Hungarian goulash and other highly seasoned meat stews.	Available whole; use mortar and pestle if ground spice is required. Perhaps the world's most ancient spice, in use since the Neolithic age.
Used primarily in Near and Far Eastern dishes; featured in curries and pilafs. Also used in cakes, custards, punches, mulled wines, pickles, and occasionally with meat, poultry and shellfish.	Expensive, and therefore seen as "festive" spice. Available whole or as seeds.

Herbs & Spices

Spice	Taste/Fragrance	Substitutions
Chili Powder	A blend of spices, usually including red pepper plus cumin, oregano, salt and garlic powder.	
Cinnamon	Warm, sweet taste and fragrance. Powdered form has stronger aroma.	An equal amount of allspice can be substituted for cinnamon, remaining in the same family of tastes. Cassia has similar flavor, more bite. It's cheaper, and often substituted for cinnamon sticks; recognizable by "double scroll" vs. single roll of true cinnamon stick.
Cloves	Ground cloves are made without the clove heads, and are milder in flavor than whole cloves.	An equal amount of allspice can be substituted for cloves, remaining in the same family of tastes.
Coriander	Seeds are warmly aromatic, mild and sweet, with citrus undertone similar to orange peel. Leaves are earthy, pungent.	From same plant, seeds are known as coriander, leaves as cilantro. Coriander is bulkiest ingredient in curry powders. Fresh cilantro is widely used in salsas, salads, and vegetable and poultry dishes.
Dill	Fruit of the parsley family. Aromatic, with spicy green taste.	

Herbs & Spices

Use in Cooking	Notes
Enhance chili powder by adding a pinch of one of the "sweet" spices: Allspice, cinnamon, cloves, or onion.	Gets its bite from capsaicin, the most pungent chemical in cayenne peppers. Capsaicin does not dissolve in water, but will dissolve in either fat or alcohol. Therefore, to cut the "fire" from eating a bowl of hot chili, drink a glass of cold milk or a chilled beer.
A favorite in baked goods, accompanies chocolate or fruit, esp. apples and pears. Use in stuffed eggplant or sweet peppers, moussaka, curries and pilafs. Also used for mulled wines, syrups, and Chinese Five Spice.	One of nature's most aromatic spices. Available in stick (quill) or powdered.
Whole cloves can be studded into an onion or carrot, or put in a tea ball for cooking; they should be removed before dish is served. Cloves are also pretty if studded in ham or pork, or in baked apples.	Make an old-fashioned pomander: Stud a fresh orange with whole cloves, let dry, and hang in your closet for a lovely scent. Cloves also help alleviate nausea while stimulating the digestive system; for clove tea, infuse about 10 whole cloves in 1 cup boiling water for 10 minutes.
Seeds are excellent in curry, tomato chutney, ratatouille, vegetables, and in soups and sauces. Great with ham and pork, esp. if orange added, or with fish and poultry. Complements chili. Also used in apple pies, pastries, gingerbread, fruitcakes, bread, and marmalade.	Cilantro is available whole or ground. It's been cultivated for over 3,000 years; seeds have been found in tombs from the 21st Egyptian dynasty (1085-945 BC). Whole seeds keep indefinitely, and improve with age. Ground coriander loses flavor and aroma quickly; store in opaque airtight container or grind as needed. Cilantro can be grown at home, and is often available fresh in markets.
Good with cucumber, cottage cheese, fish, pickles, bean soups, potatoes, tomatoes, salads & herb butter or bread.	Available as whole seeds, ground or leaves.

Herbs & Spices

Spice	Taste/Fragrance	Substitutions
Fennel	Tiny yellow-brown seeds with licorice flavor.	
Garlic	Strong, well known flavor.	
Ginger	Pungent fragrance and warm, spicy taste.	
Lemon	Lemon zest (the grated yellow portion of the peel) has a stronger flavor than lemon juice.	1 tsp. lemon zest has flavor equal to 2 tsp. candied lemon peel.
Marjoram	Mint family, with aromatic odor and distinctive savory flavor. Oregano has similar, slightly stronger flavor.	Using same type (fresh for fresh or dried for dried), ½ tsp. oregano equals flavor of 1 tsp. marjoram.
Mint	Strong sweet odor and tangy, cool taste.	
Nasturtium	Leaves have spicy, peppery flavor similar to botanical cousin, watercress.	Both seeds and leaves get their flavor from mustard oils. Pickled seeds reminiscent of capers.
Nutmeg	Sweet, nutty aroma, with nutty, warm, slightly bitter flavor.	An equal amount of allspice can be substituted for nutmeg, remaining in the same family of tastes. The outer shell of the nutmeg seed is commonly known as mace, used in cooking.

Herbs & Spices

Use in Cooking	Notes
Good with soups, fish, sauces, sweet pickles, and breads.	Available whole or ground. Excellent digestive aid.
Mash with butter and bake in French bread or spread on grilled meat or fish. Insert sliced cloves into joints of meat before roasting.	Rub cut clove around salad bowl to subtly flavor salads.
Peel & slice/grate fresh ginger for stews, sauces, and Asian dishes. Use ground ginger with poultry, and in cakes, cookies, mulled wine, and of course, gingerbread.	Freshly grated ginger infused alone or sprinkled in other teas will help relieve nausea. Available fresh or ground.
To make lemon-flavored sugar, grate enough lemon peel to make 1 TBL zest. Stir into 1 cup granulated sugar and store, tightly covered, in cool dry place.	Use only lemon-colored part of the peel; the white "pith" underneath is bitter.
Enhances pasta, eggs, cheese dishes, fish chowders, stews, roast chicken, beef, lamb, pork stuffing, & vegetable soups. Also tomatoes, zucchini, potatoes & peppers.	Makes an aromatic tea. Available fresh or dried.
Suits lamb, potatoes, peas, jellies, cakes & frostings, candies, fruit juices, ice cream & chocolate desserts.	Dried leaf of peppermint or spearmint plant. Available whole (dried), flaked or as fresh sprigs.
Leaves, flowers and stems can be used in salads. Flowers also make colorful garnish for cheese boards, vegetables, and desserts.	Eat only plants that have not been chemically treated. Like marigolds, onions, garlic and radish, nasturtiums have strong aroma that repels many garden pests, and is natural insect repellent that is not harmful to people or pets.
Excellent in pies, puddings, custards and cakes. Also combines well with soufflés, cheese or onion sauces. Comlements egg dishes, broccoli, spinach, sausages, and Italian sweet dishes. Traditionally sprinkled over eggnog.	Available whole or ground. Nutmeg is slightly poisonous, and should therefore be used in moderation. It is included in mincemeat spice, pudding spice, pastry spice, and Indian garam marsala. It also increases the potency of alcohol.

Herbs & Spices

Spice	Taste/Fragrance	Substitutions
Oregano	Mint family, with strong odor and pleasantly bitter taste. Marjoram has similar, slightly weaker flavor.	Using same type (fresh for fresh or dried for dried), 1½ tsp. marjoram equals flavor of 1 tsp. oregano.
Parsley	Mild, slightly tangy flavor. Enhances flavor of other herbs in cooking.	To increase potency of fresh parsley, use stems also, which are more strongly flavored.
Pepper	Black and white peppers taste the same.	Use white pepper when the remainder of the ingredients in a dish are light-colored (such as scalloped potatoes).
Rosemary	Aromatic resinous odor, with bittersweet, slightly piney taste.	
Saffron	Strongly perfumed, with penetrating honeyed aroma. Pungent, bitter-honey flavor.	Turmeric can be used as an inexpensive substitute, but use very little, as its acrid flavor can easily overwhelm the food.
Sage	In mint family; aromatic, with strong, warm, slightly bitter taste.	

Use in Cooking	Notes
Goes especially will with pizza and Italian dishes. Also tomato sauces, pork & veal dishes, vegetable salads, and chili.	Available fresh or dried.
Use with meats, vegetables, soups, eggs, and cheese. Fry whole sprigs briefly to serve with fish. Combine with bay leaf and thyme for bouquet garni.	Available fresh, whole, ground, or as dried flakes. When fresh, add towards the end of cooking. One of the fines herbes with chervil and tarragon.
Heightens flavor of dishes made with allspice, cloves or cinnamon, giving it a pleasant bite. Add a pinch to hot chocolate, eggnog, spiced wine punch, apple pie, baked apples or applesauce, baked pears or gingerbread.	Grind peppercorns just before use; whole peppercorns hold their flavor much better than ground pepper. Can be stored in freezer and ground while frozen. Best to grind in metal or plastic peppermill, since wood absorbs oils and is harder to keep fresh. Pepper is natural insecticide, often more toxic than pyrethrins. To protect plants, spray with solution of ½ tsp. ground pepper to one quart warm water.
Good with poultry stuffing, veal, pork and lamb roasts, pâtés, fish, duck, potatoes & cauliflower. Put whole sprig in oven to flavor baking bread.	Very pungent herb; as little as ⅛ to ¼ tsp. of fresh or dried rosemary will season a dish serving four. Aids in digestion of fats. Crumble dried leaves or chop fresh ones; if used whole, leaves must be removed after cooking, as they can be tough. Whole sprigs can be frozen to use as needed.
Crush threads before use. Infuse in hot milk or liquid from recipe, or add to flour for cakes. Used most often with rice or in pilafs. Good with fish and seafood, and in paella & bouillabaisse.	Most expensive seasoning, since it must be harvested from the inner part of a small crocus. Just a pinch will color & flavor a large dish. Good saffron should be less than a year old, and brilliant orange in color. Available whole (threads) or powdered.
Good with stuffing, poultry, sausages, hamburgers, pork roasts, breads, and omelettes.	Sage's pungency complements strongly flavored foods. Aids in the digestion of fats. If dried, sage must be top quality or it acquires unpleasant, musty flavor.

Herbs & Spices

Spice	Taste/Fragrance	Substitutions
Summer & Winter Savory	In mint family. Aromatic & pungent.	Similar flavor to thyme, with winter savory slightly milder than summer savory.
Tarragon	Aristocratic herb with mild flavor and hidden tang. Pungent, resembling licorice.	
Thyme	Member of mint family; warm aroma & pungent flavor.	One sprig fresh thyme equals the flavoring power of ½ tsp. ground dried thyme. Thyme leaves are sweetest if picked just as the flowers appear.

Compiled using information from:

The Complete Book of Herbs, Spices and Condiments,
by Carol Ann Rinzler, Facts On File, New York * Oxford, 1990.

Cooking with Spices, by Carolyn Heal and Michael Allsop, David & Charles, Ltd., 1983.

Herbs, Lesley Bremness, Dorling Kindersley Ltd, London, 1990.

Herbs: Their Cultivation and Usage,
by John and Rosemary Hemphill, Sterling Publishing Co., Inc., New York, 1989

Herbs & Spices

Use in Cooking	Notes
Cook with fresh/dried beans or lentils, or in white sauce for bean dishes. Mix with parsley & chives for roasting duck. Sprinkle finely chopped leaves on soups & sauces. Use with eggs, meat, chicken, salads, & stuffing.	Available whole or ground.
Indispensable for béarnaise and hollandaise sauces. Good with fish, chicken, sauces for meats, delicate vegetables, green salads, tomatoes, egg & cheese dishes, pickles, vinegar, and soups.	One of the fines herbes with chervil and parsley. Available fresh, whole or ground. Freezing fresh leaves preserves their flavoring oils, whereas drying evaporates them. Frozen leaves will keep in freezer for 3-5 months; no need to defrost before use.
Good with stuffing, meat, shellfish, and game, also eggs, cheese, bean & vegetable soups, & clam chowders. Try lemon thyme with poultry and fish.	Used in bouquet garni with bay leaf and parsley. Stimulates the appetite and aids in the digestion of fats. Very pungent when fresh, so use with discretion. Available fresh, whole or powdered. If scattered around your linen closet, dried thyme leaves will scent the closet and repel insects.

Notes

Do–Si–Do ~ Accompaniments

Above: Point-to-Point at Winterthur

Right: Tailgating at Point-to-Point

Do–Si–Do
Accompaniments

Point-to-Point at Winterthur

The Winterthur Point-to-Point steeplechase is a fundraiser that attracts thousands of spectators to an elegant day full of equestrian activities. In addition to the horse races, highlights include an antique carriage parade, tailgate picnic competition (shown here), children's activities, and dog obedience shows. This annual Brandywine valley tradition takes place on Sunday of the first full weekend in May.

Photograph by Victoria Novak,
courtesy of Winterthur

Tailgating at Point-to-Point

This sophisticated social event wouldn't be the same without the Tailgate Competition. Individuals create lavish displays to compete for wonderful prizes, in categories ranging from best theme to best entrée and best dessert. The theme is new each year, and winners are judged by local celebrities and restaurateurs.

Photograph courtesy of
Winterthur

Broccoli Amandine

Serves 6 to 8

2 pounds fresh broccoli, cut into florets
Salt and freshly ground black pepper to taste
½ stick (4 tablespoons) butter
1 ounce sliced almonds
1 clove minced garlic
¼ cup freshly squeezed lemon juice

Rinse the broccoli and season with salt and pepper. Place the broccoli in a basket set over boiling water, cover tightly, and steam until crisp-tender, about 5 minutes. Melt the butter in a small sauté pan. Add the almonds and garlic, and cook until the nuts are golden. Place the broccoli in a serving dish, drizzle with the almond-garlic mixture, and add the lemon juice. Toss lightly to mix; serve immediately.

To toast slivered or sliced almonds, spread in a shallow pan and bake in a 350°F oven until lightly browned, 7 to 9 minutes, stirring frequently.

Brussels Sprouts in Pecan Butter

Serves 4

1 pound fresh Brussels sprouts
½ stick (4 tablespoons) butter
4 ounces chopped pecans
Salt and freshly ground black pepper to taste

Trim and make an X in the bottom of each sprout with a paring knife. Cook in boiling, salted water until tender, about 10 minutes. Drain the sprouts and hold in a warm oven. Melt the butter in a large sauté pan over medium heat until light brown. Stir in the pecans. Gently stir in the sprouts, coating well with the pecan-butter mixture. Season with salt and pepper. Serve immediately.

The hostess must be like the duck: Calm and unruffled on the surface, and paddling like hell underneath.

~ Anonymous

Butter Braised Leeks

Serves 4

8 leeks, about 1 inch in diameter
4 tablespoons butter
Salt to taste
¼ cup freshly grated Parmesan cheese

To prepare the leeks, cut off the roots and the coarse part of the green, leaving about 7 inches total. Cut in half lengthwise, then into 2-inch sections. Wash well in a colander under cold running water to remove all dirt and grit. Drain well and pat dry.

Melt the butter in a skillet with a lid over medium-low heat. Add the leeks. Cover and cook for 12 to 15 minutes, stirring once or twice. When just tender, uncover, increase the heat to medium-high, and let the liquid evaporate almost completely. Leeks should brown slightly. Salt to taste and sprinkle with Parmesan. Stir to coat and place on a warmed platter to serve.

Grilled Asparagus

Serves 4

1 pound asparagus, woody ends snapped or trimmed
3 tablespoons balsamic vinegar
2 tablespoons freshly squeezed lemon juice
1 tablespoon olive oil
1 tablespoon soy sauce
Pinch of crushed red pepper flakes

Combine all the ingredients in a plastic zipperlock bag. Marinate 30 minutes in the refrigerator. Coat a grill rack with cooking spray and prepare the grill to a medium-high heat. Grill 5 minutes, or until crisp-tender. Do not overcook.

♪ *Great summertime picnic dish served with BBQ or grilled meats. May also marinate red peppers and pineapple for a colorful grilled vegetable side dish.*

Asparagus Wrapped with Prosciutto

Serves 8 to 10

1 large bunch asparagus, trimmed

2 tablespoons unsalted butter

8 ounces fresh morel or chanterelle mushrooms, trimmed, rinsed, and patted dry

1 teaspoon minced garlic

1 tablespoon minced fresh tarragon leaves

6 ounces thinly sliced prosciutto

Bring a large pot of lightly salted water to a boil. Place the asparagus in the water and blanch about 4 to 6 minutes, or until crisp-tender. Remove the asparagus from the water and pat dry.

Melt the butter in a large skillet over medium heat. Add the mushrooms and sauté until they have softened and started to release some of their liquid, about 4 minutes. Add the garlic and cook for 1 minute. Remove from heat and stir in the tarragon.

To serve, wrap 3 asparagus stalks with a slice of prosciutto to make a bundle. Repeat with remaining asparagus and prosciutto. Place on a serving platter and spoon the warm mushrooms over the top.

Nasturtium flowers and leaves are edible. They have a peppery taste that lends itself to flavoring vegetables and salads, while they add a splash of color to the plate.

~

To perk up your vegetables, add ½ teaspoon salt and ½ teaspoon sugar to the boiling water before adding the vegetables.

Green Beans with Lemon and Onion

Serves 6 to 8

3 pounds green beans, trimmed

6 tablespoons butter

1 onion, finely chopped

Juice of 1 lemon

Salt and freshly ground black pepper to taste

Cook the beans in a large pot of boiling, lightly salted water just until crisp-tender. Drain in a colander and rinse under cold running water to stop the cooking process. Melt the butter in a skillet over medium-high heat. Add the onion and cook until soft, about 5 minutes. (The dish can be made ahead up to this point.) Just before serving, reheat the onion on medium. Add the beans and lemon juice, tossing to coat. Warm until just heated through. Season with salt and pepper.

Fresh Asparagus Risotto
Serves 4 to 6

1½ cups asparagus, woody ends trimmed and discarded, tips removed and reserved, and stalks cut diagonally into ½ inch slices

5 cups low-sodium, fat-free chicken broth

2 tablespoons extra virgin olive oil

3 tablespoons unsalted butter, divided

1 shallot, minced (about 2 tablespoons)

1 cup Arborio rice

¼ cup dry Italian vermouth or dry white wine

½ cup freshly grated Parmigiano-Reggiano cheese

Salt and freshly ground black pepper to taste

Known in the 18th century as Cantwell's Bridge, Odessa was a busy grain shipping port. Today, the town has tree-lined streets and 18th and 19th century homes, many of which were restored by H. Rodney Sharp. Historic Houses of Odessa offers tours of four of these homes, as well as living history demonstrations of open hearth cooking and kitchen gardening (seasonally), and spring and Yuletide tours.

Prepare an ice bath in a large bowl. Blanch the asparagus stalks (but not the tips) in a large pot of boiling, salted water until bright green, then remove immediately and plunge into the ice bath to stop the cooking process. Drain the stalks and repeat the process with the tips.

Bring the broth to a simmer in a small saucepan, adjusting the heat so that the broth continues to simmer. Heat a 6-quart saucepan on medium-high and add the oil and 2 tablespoons of the butter. Sauté the shallot until softened and translucent. Add the rice and sauté, stirring constantly, until the rice is coated with the oil. Add the vermouth and cook, stirring, until the vermouth is almost completely absorbed. Using a ladle, begin adding the hot broth, about a ½ cup at a time, stirring constantly with a wooden spoon. Allow the rice to almost completely absorb the liquid before adding more broth. When a little more than half the broth has been added, stir in the asparagus stalks (but not the tips). Continue adding the broth. When there is only about ½ cup of broth remaining, add the asparagus tips. Add the remaining tablespoon of butter and the Parmesan cheese, stirring vigorously to blend. Serve immediately.

♪ *Risotto is a time consuming dish, but well worth the time. A pressure cooker can reduce the cooking time to about 12 minutes. The asparagus preparation is the same; just follow the pressure cooker instructions for the risotto. This makes a great side dish or main course.*

Gingered Green Beans

Serves 4 to 6

1 tablespoon butter
1½ tablespoons peeled and minced fresh ginger
2 cloves garlic, minced
½ cup pecans, chopped
3 tablespoons lite soy sauce
2 tablespoons sherry
1¼ pound green beans, trimmed

Melt the butter in large skillet over medium-high heat. Sauté the ginger, garlic, and pecans for 3 minutes, or until the pecans are toasted. Transfer to a small bowl and set aside. Add the soy sauce, sherry, and green beans to the skillet. Cover and simmer for 15 to 20 minutes, stirring occasionally until the beans are cooked. Remove from the heat and toss in the pecan mixture, coating thoroughly before serving.

Kahlúa Glazed Carrots

Serves 6

3 cups carrots sliced on the diagonal
1 tablespoon butter or margarine
1 tablespoon brown sugar
1 tablespoon honey
3 tablespoons Kahlúa or other coffee-flavored liqueur, divided
1 teaspoon cornstarch
¼ teaspoon salt
3 slices bacon, cooked and crumbled
1 tablespoon chopped fresh parsley leaves

Place the carrots in a vegetable steamer over a small amount of boiling water. Cover tightly and steam 4 to 5 minutes, or until crisp-tender. Remove from the heat and uncover. Melt the butter in a large skillet over medium heat. Stir in brown sugar, honey, and 2 tablespoons of the Kahlúa; cook over medium heat until bubbly. Combine the remaining 1 tablespoon of Kahlúa with the cornstarch; stir well and add to brown sugar mixture. Stir in the salt. Continue cooking until thickened and bubbly. Add the carrots, tossing gently to coat, and cook just until the carrots are thoroughly heated. Spoon into a serving dish. Sprinkle with crumbled bacon and chopped parsley.

To peel fresh ginger, remove the brown papery skin with a small paring knife or vegetable peeler. Peeled ginger can be chopped with a chef's knife, or in a food processor fitted with the metal blade. To grate, draw peeled ginger across the fine holes of a metal, bamboo, or porcelain ginger grater.

For an elegant centerpiece, arrange sugared fruits in a shallow bowl. To sugar fruit, dip it into lightly beaten egg whites, roll it gently in a bowl of granulated sugar, and set aside on paper towels to dry for several hours. Red and white grapes, pears and strawberries work particularly well.

Curried Cauliflower

Serves 6

2 tablespoons vegetable oil
1 teaspoon black or brown mustard seeds
2 teaspoons peeled and minced fresh ginger
1 teaspoon ground coriander seeds
½ teaspoon turmeric
½ teaspoon ground cardamom
Pinch of cayenne pepper
1 medium-size head cauliflower, cut into florets of equal size
½ cup unsweetened apple juice
2 tablespoons freshly squeezed lemon juice
Salt to taste
Yogurt (optional)
Currants (optional)

Heat a large skillet on high and add the oil. Add the mustard seeds and cook until they begin to pop, about 30 seconds. Stir in the ginger, coriander, turmeric, cardamom, and cayenne. Add the cauliflower and toss with the spices. Pour in the apple juice and lemon juice, and season with salt. Cover and simmer until the cauliflower is just tender, about 5 minutes, stirring occasionally. Serve hot or at room temperature. Or, serve cold with a dollop of plain yogurt and 2 tablespoons currants, for garnish.

Tomato Concassé

Serves 4

3 or 4 medium-size ripe tomatoes (6 to 8 ounces each)
¼ to ½ cup extra virgin olive oil
Splash of sherry vinegar
Combination of fresh basil, cilantro, chives, dill, or parsley leaves, chopped
Salt to taste

Cut out the top core of the tomatoes and make an X in the bottom of each one to make peeling easier. Blanch in boiling water for about 15 seconds, then rinse under cool water. Peel the tomatoes. Discard the seeds and center of the tomato. Finely dice the flesh. Combine the diced tomato with extra virgin olive oil, sherry vinegar, and a combination of the fresh herbs in a medium bowl. Toss lightly and store up to 3 hours before using. Just before serving, season with salt.

♪ *A spoonful of tomato concassé is wonderful with chicken or grilled fish, or as a topping for pasta, summer soups, or bruschetta.*

Chicken or vegetable broth perks up soups and stews, and also adds great flavor to rice, grits and mashed potatoes. Use instead of water, and reduce salt accordingly.

Spinach and Rice

Serves 4

1⅓ cups uncooked quick rice
3 tablespoons butter or margarine
¼ cup chopped onion
¼ cup water
½ cup sliced water chestnuts
½ teaspoon salt
⅛ teaspoon freshly ground black pepper
1 (10 ounce) package frozen chopped spinach
2 tablespoons freshly grated Parmesan cheese

Cook the rice according to package directions. Heat a medium skillet on medium-high. Melt the butter and sauté the onion until tender, but not browned. Stir in the water, water chestnuts, salt, and pepper. Stir the onion mixture into the cooked rice. Cook the spinach and drain well, squeezing to remove as much water as possible. Stir the spinach into the rice mixture and reheat until warmed through. Spoon into a warm serving dish and sprinkle with Parmesan.

*If dinner must wait,
you can keep cooked rice hot
and fluffy in the pan by
laying a slice of dry bread
on top, then clapping
on the lid.*

Summer Vegetable Rice Pilaf

Serves 6

1 cup long-grain brown rice, rinsed well

2½ cups water

2 teaspoons olive oil

1 large onion, chopped

2 cloves garlic, finely chopped

1 zucchini, diced

1 red bell pepper, diced

1½ cups fresh or frozen corn niblets

1 (4 ounce) can mild green chiles, drained and chopped

¼ cup chopped fresh cilantro or parsley leaves

¼ teaspoon freshly ground black pepper

¼ teaspoon dried basil or 3 to 4 tablespoons chopped fresh basil leaves

¼ teaspoon coriander

¼ pound feta cheese, crumbled

Combine the rice and water in a medium saucepan, and bring to a boil. Reduce the heat to low, cover, and cook gently for about 40 minutes, or until the water is absorbed and the rice is cooked. Heat a large, deep skillet on medium-high. Add the oil and sauté the onion and garlic for about 5 minutes, or until the onion is translucent. Add the zucchini and cook for 5 minutes. Add the red pepper, corn, and chiles; continue to cook for 5 to 10 minutes more. Stir in the cilantro, pepper, basil, and coriander. Remove from the heat. Preheat the oven to 325°F. When the rice is cooked, reheat the vegetable mixture and stir in the rice and feta cheese. Place in a casserole dish and bake for 15 minutes.

Wild Rice, Raisins, and Pecans

Serves 6

1⅓ cups long-grain and wild rice combined
5½ cups chicken broth
1 cup chopped pecans
1 cup golden raisins
½ orange zest, finely grated
⅓ cup orange juice, pulp removed
¼ cup olive oil
3 sprigs fresh mint leaves, finely chopped
1½ teaspoons salt, or more to taste

Rinse the rice under cold water. Combine the rice with the chicken broth in a medium saucepan and bring to a boil. Reduce the heat, cover, and simmer for 30 to 45 minutes, or until the rice is tender. Drain the rice and let cool. Combine the pecans, raisins, orange zest, orange juice, olive oil, mint, and salt in a large bowl. Stir in the cooled rice and let stand for approximately 1½ hours for the flavors to meld. Serve at room temperature.

♪ *This recipe can be used as a salad or a wonderful side dish to prepare ahead of time. Delicious with pork or chicken.*

Macaroni and Cheese

Serves 6

1½ cups uncooked macaroni
¾ pound extra sharp Cheddar cheese, shredded
1½ teaspoons dry mustard
3¾ cups of milk
1¼ teaspoons salt
3 eggs, slightly beaten

Preheat the oven to 350°F. Spray a 9 x 13 baking dish with nonstick cooking oil. Cook the macaroni in a large pot of boiling, salted water until al dente. Combine the mustard and milk in a large bowl. Add the eggs, mixing well. Stir in the macaroni and cheese, saving out enough cheese to sprinkle over the top. Pour the mixture into the baking dish and top with the remaining cheese. Bake for 30 minutes, or until the cheese is melted and bubbly.

Prime Hook National Wildlife Refuge, located on the western shore of the Delaware Bay, 22 miles southeast of Dover, hosts spectacular concentrations of migrating waterfowl during the spring and fall. The refuge consists of over 9,700 acres, three-quarters of which is freshwater marsh, tidal marsh, and open water; other habitats include woods, grasslands, and croplands.

The fall migration brings birdwatchers to see Canada and snow geese, and a wide assortment of ducks, while May is the best time for viewing shorebirds and warblers. Many types of wading birds, terns and songbirds add to the variety, and large numbers of waterfowl winter on the refuge as well. Visitors also enjoy nature trails, fishing and hunting in season, photography, boating and more than seven miles of canoe trails.

To keep potatoes from budding, place an apple in the bag with them.

~

The word "salary" comes from Roman times, when salt was so precious it was used as cash.

Potato Gratin with Swiss and Cheddar Cheese

Serves 6

2 pounds baking potatoes, peeled and thinly sliced
2 teaspoons minced garlic
1 teaspoon salt, divided
½ teaspoon white pepper, divided
1 cup heavy cream
½ cup grated Swiss cheese
½ cup grated Cheddar cheese

Preheat the oven to 375°F. Place half of the potato slices in an ungreased 9 x 9 x 2-inch square baking dish. Sprinkle with half of the garlic, salt, and pepper. Cover with the remaining potatoes, and sprinkle with the remaining garlic, salt, and pepper. Pour the cream over potatoes. Cover tightly with foil and bake 1 hour, or until the potatoes are tender. Increase the oven temperature to 450°F. Uncover the potatoes and top with the cheeses. Bake uncovered until the cheese melts, about 10 minutes. Cool slightly before serving to let set.

♪ *Outstanding with beef or lamb.*

A Cook's Guide to Potatoes

Name	Type	Best Uses
Bintje	White	French fries, hash browns
Russet	White	Baked & Mashed
Charlotte	Gold	Steamed & boiled
Russian Banana	Gold fingerling	Roasted, boiled & sautéed
Yukon Gold	Gold	Mashed
Red Bliss	Red	Roasted & in potato salad
All Blue	Blue	Mashed, gratinéed & baked
Purple Peruvian	Purple	Potato salad

Mashed Potato Casserole

Serves 8 to 10

10 to 12 medium potatoes, peeled and diced
1 (8 ounce) package cream cheese
1 cup sour cream
Salt and freshly ground black pepper to taste
¼ cup chives
1 cup milk, or more as needed
¼ cup butter, melted

Preheat the oven to 350°F. Grease a 13 x 9-inch casserole dish. Cook the potatoes in boiling water until tender. Drain and mash coarsely. Add the cream cheese, sour cream, salt, pepper, and chives. Add the milk, a little at a time until the desired consistency is reached. Place the mixture into the casserole dish. Pour the butter over the potatoes and bake for 25 to 30 minutes, or until golden brown. (Alternatively, microwave until heated through.)

♪ *This dish can be made ahead of time and reheated when ready to serve.*

Holiday Sweet Potatoes

Serves 6 to 8

Casserole

3 cups cooked sweet potatoes, mashed
½ cup butter or margarine
1 cup sugar
1 teaspoon pure vanilla extract
½ cup milk
2 eggs, beaten

Topping

⅓ cup butter or margarine, at room temperature
1 cup firmly packed light brown sugar
⅓ cup flour
1 cup chopped pecans

Preheat the oven to 375°F. Combine all the ingredients for the casserole and pour into an 8-inch square baking dish. To prepare the topping, cream the butter and the brown sugar together. Add the flour and pecans, mixing well. Crumble the topping on top of the casserole and bake for 30 minutes. Serve warm.

Accompaniments

Potatoes

American potatoes fall into four basic categories: Russets, long whites, round reds and round whites.

~ RUSSETS have rough brown skins and mealy flesh; they are best for baking and mashing.

~ LONG WHITES have moist waxy flesh, which makes them great boiled, baked or fried.

~ ROUND REDS and ROUND WHITES are thin-skinned with less starch and more moisture; while perfect for boiling, they also do well when roasted or fried.

~ NEW POTATOES are simply the "babies" of any of these varieties.

The same spirit of freedom that made Delaware "The First State," fueled a powerful opposition to slavery from the start of the Republic through the Civil War. Delaware became an important stop on the Underground Railroad, helping transport slaves escaping to freedom in the north. In 1854, Quaker merchant Thomas Garrett came before the U.S. Supreme Court, sued by a Maryland slave-owner for aiding a black family in flight. Garrett was fined $5,400, virtually his entire fortune. Undaunted, he pledged to fight on against slavery. Over his life, he reportedly helped more than 2,000 fugitive slaves and is thought to be the model for a Quaker farmer in Uncle Tom's Cabin.

Apple Cranberry Casserole

Serves 10 to 12

Casserole

3 tablespoons flour
1 cup sugar
5 cups peeled and chopped Granny Smith apples
1 (12 ounce) package fresh cranberries, washed and cut in half

Topping

2 envelopes instant cinnamon-spice oatmeal
¾ cup chopped pecans or walnuts
½ cup all-purpose flour
½ cup packed light brown sugar
½ cup melted butter

Preheat the oven to 350°F. Grease a 9 x 13-inch casserole dish. To prepare the casserole, combine the flour and sugar together in a large, sealable bowl. Add the apples and cranberries, and shake gently until coated. Place the apple mixture into the casserole. To prepare the topping, combine all the ingredients and crumble over the casserole. Bake for about 45 minutes.

♪ *This recipe can be served as a side dish with turkey or ham, or with vanilla ice cream for dessert.*

Apple-Onion Bake

Serves 6 to 8

6 apples, peeled and thinly sliced
2 red onions, thinly sliced
¾ cup packed light brown sugar
¼ cup butter or margarine
Bread crumbs for topping

Preheat the oven to 375°F. Layer the apples and onion in a 2-quart baking dish. Sprinkle with brown sugar and dot with butter. Repeat the layers about 3 times. (The apples will mound up over the baking dish, but will cook down.) Sprinkle the bread crumbs over top. Bake for 30 or 45 minutes, or until the apples and onions are tender.

♪ *This is a very unusual, old New England recipe,*
that always gets rave reviews.

Pineapple Casserole

Serves 6 to 8

1 (1 pound) can crushed pineapple, in its own juice, partially drained
½ cup sugar
4 heaping teaspoons cornstarch
½ stick melted butter
4 eggs, slightly beaten

Preheat the oven to 350°F. Combine all the ingredients in a large bowl with an electric mixer. Pour into an ungreased casserole dish and bake for 45 minutes, or until set in the center. Serve hot or cold.

♪ *Delicious, quick, and easy. Tastes great with ham.*

Garrett's unstinting devotion to the cause of freedom is the subject of two exhibits at the historic New Castle Courthouse. More information is given at Wilmington's Quaker Hill, the city's first residential neighborhood, as well as one of the final stops on the Underground Railroad. The Garrett-Tubman Riverfront Park is named in honor of Garrett and Harriett Tubman, the famed abolitionist who worked closely with Delaware's anti-slavery forces.

Calico Squash

Serves 8

2 cups sliced yellow squash
1 cup sliced zucchini
1 medium onion, chopped
¼ cup sliced scallions
1 cup water
2 cups crushed Ritz crackers
½ cup butter or margarine, melted
1 (10¾ ounce) can cream of celery soup
1 (8 ounce) can sliced water chestnuts
1 large carrot, grated
1 jar diced pimentos
1 teaspoon chopped dried sage
½ cup mayonnaise
1 cup shredded Cheddar cheese

Preheat the oven to 350°F. Combine the squash, zucchini, onion, and scallions in a medium saucepan. Add the water and bring to a boil for about 6 minutes. Combine the crackers and melted butter in small bowl. In another bowl, combine the celery soup, water chestnuts, carrot, pimentos, sage, and mayonnaise. Stir in the squash-zucchini mixture to the soup mixture.

Pat half of the crumb mixture into the bottom of a casserole dish. Spoon the squash mixture over the crumbs. Sprinkle with the cheese and top with the remaining crumbs. Bake for 30 minutes until lightly browned.

Baked Peppers

Serves 12

3 red bell peppers, halved and seeded
3 yellow bell peppers, halved and seeded
Olive oil
2 cloves garlic, crushed
1 pint red cherry tomatoes
1 pint yellow cherry tomatoes
3 tablespoons capers
Freshly grated Parmesan cheese to taste

Preheat the oven to 400°F. Arrange the red and yellow peppers in a baking pan, cut-side up, and rub the inside of each with the garlic and olive oil. Fill the red pepper halves with yellow tomatoes and yellow peppers halves with red tomatoes. Sprinkle with capers and drizzle with additional olive oil. Bake for 35 minutes. Sprinkle with Parmesan cheese and serve immediately.

Corn Pudding

Serves 4 to 6

3 tablespoons butter, softened
2 tablespoons sugar
2 tablespoons flour
1 teaspoon salt
3 eggs, slightly beaten
2 cups frozen corn kernels, chopped coarsely
1¾ cups milk

Preheat the oven to 325°F. Grease a 9 x 13-inch casserole dish. Combine the butter, sugar, flour, and salt in a large bowl. Add the eggs and beat well. Stir in the corn and milk. Pour the mixture into the casserole dish. Bake, stirring once halfway through, for 45 minutes, or until the pudding is golden brown on top and a knife inserted in the middle comes out clean.

Harrington Raceway in Sussex County is the oldest continually operated harness racetrack in America.

~

The first scheduled steam railroad in the nation began in New Castle, Delaware, in 1831.

Mushroom Varieties

~ *Button mushrooms* are the most popular, all-purpose mushroom, with a delicate flavor and crisp, firm texture. They range in color from snow white through pale ivory to brown, and vary in size from tiny buttons to medium and large. Their fresh mushroom flavor intensifies as the mushroom matures. They are the most widely cultivated mushrooms in the world.

~ *Chanterelles* are gold or apricot trumpets ranging from bite-sized to 5 or 6 inches. They are considered to be one of the two or three finest culinary mushrooms. When fresh, they are mildly mushroomy, with a nutty, peppery, cinnamony, or apricot-like taste, sometimes reminiscent of shellfish. The dried form is very expensive; when reconstituted, their texture is chewy and their flavor delicate. They are wonderful paired with chicken, eggs or seafood; sauté gently and glaze them with meat juices or their own liquid.

~ *Creminis* have a dark brown exterior and beige interior. They are very flavorful and have a denser, meatier texture than ordinary white button mushrooms. The Crimini's special flavor enhances any sauce in which mushrooms are used. They can be sautéed, grilled, broiled or baked. Because of their size and firmness, they are the ideal mushrooms for stuffing. Their shelf life is one week.

~ *Enoki (Ee-no-kee) mushrooms* originally were found growing on dead trees in Japan. They are grown and packaged in small clusters and are creamy white in color. Enokis have a mild flavor, a long slender stem and tiny caps. They are best eaten raw in salads and sandwiches, or as a garnish atop soups. When preparing Enoki mushrooms, trim roots at the base and separate stems before serving. Their shelf life is 3 to 4 days.

~ *Morels* are pale yellowish tan to dark gray, with a honeycombed conical shape and hollow stem and core unique among mushrooms. They range in size from 1 to 5 inches. When fresh, their flavor is delicately nutty and mushroomy. Their wonderful, waffle-textured caps are perfect for absorbing sauces. Dried morels are more intensely mushroom flavored, with a smoky quality. Raw morels can cause an upset stomach, so they are best cooked.

For a quick fall centerpiece, fill a pretty bowl with a combination of brightly colored bell peppers. After the party, you can use them in your favorite recipes ~ try our Black Bean and Rice Salad!

~ *Oyster mushrooms* are delicate and fan-shaped, clustered together to resemble an exotic creature of the sea. Their texture and flavor are equally delicate, and subtly suggestive of seafood. Oyster mushrooms, with their silky consistency and graceful appearance, complement any seafood dish, as well as omelets, salads, soups and sauces. They can be used in recipes as a substitute for white button mushrooms, but should be added during the final stages of cooking in order to keep their velvety texture. Their shelf life is 2 to 3 days.

~ *Porcinis* are intensely earthy and woodsy tasting ~ if chanterelles are violins, these are cellos. Their large, puffy caps sit on bulbous stems, hence the name, which means "little pigs." Fresh porcini mushrooms can be grilled or briefly sautéed to preserve their meaty texture, or slowly braised to extract their deep flavor. Dried and reconstituted, porcinis are used to flavor sauces, soups and stews, which they do better than less assertive mushrooms. These mushrooms spoil quickly, and should be eaten, or cooked and frozen, within a day or two.

~ *Portabellas* have a long growing cycle, which produces a mushroom with a very substantial texture and deep meaty flavor. Long thin slices of Portabella mushrooms are a delicious addition to stir fry dishes, or they can be breaded and deep fried as an unusual entrée. They also make a terrific meat substitute: When grilled, they taste like steak! The impressive appearance of the Portabella lends itself to interesting interpretations by innovative chefs. Its shelf life is one week.

~ *Shiitake (she-TAH-keh) mushrooms* were once an exclusive delicacy grown outdoors in the Orient. Distinctively woodsy or smoky in flavor, this versatile cultivated specialty mushroom stands up to red meat and stands out in sauces, soups and stir-fries. Use only the spongy, full-bodied caps, discarding the fibrous tough stems. Its shelf life is one week.

Kennett Square, Pennsylvania, is known as "The Mushroom Capital of the World." Back in 1896, two local nurserymen, Harry Hicks and William Swayne, figured out how to construct a building where temperatures and ventilation could be controlled in order to grow mushrooms commercially. Today, 25% of the mushrooms produced in the United States come from Kennett Square.

Due to Delaware's unique incorporation laws, over half of the Fortune 500 companies in the U.S. are incorporated in the state of Delaware. Delaware's Chancery Court is widely recognized as the nation's preeminent forum for settling disputes involving corporations and other business entities.

Mushrooms
Tips on Selection, Use and Storage

~ One pound of fresh mushrooms is equivalent to approximately 6 cups sliced or 5 cups chopped. Sliced and cooked, one pound of mushrooms yields approximately 1¾ cups.

~ Purchase mushrooms that are moist and plump, neither dry and shriveled nor wet and slimy, and without soft, discolored spots. Remove promptly from airtight wrappings, or they will quickly become slippery and inedible. The exception is enokis, which should remain sealed until use.

~ Refrigerate mushrooms in a single layer, on a shallow tray lined with paper towels. To prevent drying and shriveling, gently drape a damp paper towel or dampened cheesecloth over the mushrooms to retain moisture.

~ Do not place mushrooms on the bottom shelf of your refrigerator or in closed bins. Good air circulation is essential.

~ High heat dissipates the subtle flavor of mushrooms. Most mushrooms are best when sautéed at medium temperature in butter or olive oil, until some of the juices just begin to run, and then simmered with added liquid ~ stock, wine or cream.

~ Mushrooms have a natural affinity for onions, garlic, leeks, shallots, and almost all herbs (but particularly marjoram), ginger, soy, mustard, Madeira and sherry, olives, anchovies, eggs, potatoes, rice and other grains, and sweet red peppers (especially with shiitakes).

~ Since mushrooms do not grow with name tags attached, and since some culinary varieties are almost indistinguishable from their lethal lookalikes, it is imperative that you not eat mushrooms from the wild without being absolutely certain what they are.

~ To store for longer periods, mushrooms can be briefly sautéed in butter or oil and then frozen for a month or two.

~ There is no need to peel cultivated mushrooms. Just trim the stems before using.

~ Never soak mushrooms in water, since they will absorb it like a sponge, which dilutes their flavor considerably. Instead, wipe with a dampened towel or clean with a mushroom brush. Quickly wash mushrooms only when absolutely necessary, then pat thoroughly dry.

Excerpted from information provided by Phillips Mushroom Farms, Kennett Square, PA, and The Mushroom Book, by Michael McLaughlin

Last Waltz ~ Desserts

Dining Room at Eleutherian Mills,
Hagley Museum

Last Waltz
Desserts

Dining Room at Eleutherian Mills, Hagley Museum

The dining room pictured here occupies the entire north wing of Hagley Museum's Eleutherian Mills, the original du Pont family home in America. It is papered with a French blockprinted wallpaper entitled "Scenic America," depicting various points of interest: Natural Bridge, Virginia; the fortification of West Point on the Hudson River; a general view of New York City and the bay from Weehauken; and a general view of Boston, the State House and harbor. The table setting varies with the season. Canton and French porcelain are displayed alternately; the French dessert service with plum-colored band is shown here. It is attributed to the factory of André Cottier, and was made during the first quarter of the nineteenth-century. The table is set with silver flatware made by Wilmington silversmith Henry J. Pepper. Hagley's Eleutherian Mills is located on the museum's upper property in Wilmington, where visitors can also see the first office of the DuPont Company, and the E.I. du Pont Restored Garden.

Photograph courtesy of
Hagley Museum

Chocolate Macaroons

Yields 4 to 5 dozen cookies

1 (12 ounce) package semi-sweet chocolate chips
¼ cup butter
2 eggs
¾ cup sugar
2 tablespoons flour
1½ cups rolled oats
1 teaspoon pure vanilla extract
1 teaspoon instant coffee granules
¾ to 1 cup coconut

Preheat the oven to 375°F. Grease a cookie sheet or set aside a nonstick cookie sheet. Melt the chocolate chips in the microwave or in a double boiler. Remove from the heat and stir in the butter. Beat the eggs until thick with an electric mixer. Add the chocolate to the eggs, and combine well with the mixer. Beat in the sugar, flour, oatmeal, vanilla, coffee, and coconut. When thoroughly combined, drop by tablespoonfuls onto the greased cookie sheet. (The macaroons can be placed fairly close together, as they do not spread.) Bake for 6 to 8 minutes, cool on wire racks, and store in an airtight container until ready to serve.

Mini Reese's Tart Cookies

Yields 72 cookies

2 rolls chocolate chip cookie dough, preferably Pillsbury
2 large bags Mini Reese's Peanut Butter Cups (72 total Reese's)

Preheat the oven to 350°F. Cut cookie roll into 9 slices, and then cut each slice into 4 pieces. Place the cookie pieces into mini tart pans. Bake for 10 minutes, and them remove from the oven immediately. Place 1 peanut butter cup into each cookie, return to the oven, and bake for 5 more minutes. Remove from the oven, and allow to cool slightly before removing the cookies from the pan.

Chocolate needs to be kept dry when melting, so it should never be covered as it melts. Also, make sure that your bowls and utensils are completely dry when working with melted chocolate. If moisture gets into the chocolate, it will "seize" and no longer be smooth. If this happens, the chocolate can still be used in cake, cookie or brownie recipes, but the texture will no longer work in frostings or candies. It is sometimes possible to "rescue" the chocolate by adding solid shortening, ½ teaspoon at a time, and stirring until smooth.

The Ultimate Chocolate Chip Cookies

Yields 6 to 8 dozen cookies

1 cup granulated sugar
1 cup packed light brown sugar
⅔ cup butter, softened
⅔ cup shortening
2 eggs
3 teaspoons pure vanilla extract
3 cups flour
1 teaspoon baking soda
1 teaspoon salt
12 ounces chocolate chips
1 cup chopped nuts (optional)

Preheat the oven to 350°F.

Combine the granulated sugar, brown sugar, butter, shortening, eggs, and vanilla in a large bowl with an electric mixer until light and fluffy. Combine the flour, baking soda, and salt in a separate bowl. Stir in to the sugar mixture. Stir in the chocolate chips and nuts, if desired.

Drop by tablespoonfuls onto ungreased cookie sheets, preferably air-bake sheets. Bake 8 to 10 minutes, or until light brown. Remove from the oven and let stand 1 minute, then remove to wire racks to allow the cookies to cool completely. Store in an airtight container until ready to serve.

To keep homemade cookies from getting hard or crunchy, place them in an airtight container with a piece of fresh bread. The cookies absorb moisture from the bread, which becomes hard and stale while the cookies remain soft and chewy. Replace the bread every other day.

~

We learn the joy of work and the gentle art of nourishing at our own hearths, with flour on our hands.

*~ Katrina Kenison
(from* Mitten Strings
For God: Reflections for
Mothers in a Hurry*)*

Amish Whoopie Pies

Yields 24 to 36 (2-inch) sandwiches

Cookies

1 cup shortening

2 cups granulated sugar

2 eggs

4 cups flour

1 cup cocoa

2 teaspoons salt

2 teaspoons baking soda

1 cup buttermilk

1 cup hot water

Filling

1 cup shortening

4 cups confectioners' sugar

4 tablespoons flour

2 egg whites, beaten

4 tablespoons milk

1 teaspoon pure vanilla extract

Preheat the oven to 350°F. Beat together the shortening and sugar with an electric mixer until creamy. Add the eggs one at a time, mixing well between each addition. Combine the flour, cocoa, salt, and baking soda in a medium bowl. Add the flour mixture to the shortening, 1 cup at a time, alternately with the buttermilk and water. Blend until well combined. Drop by equal tablespoonfuls onto cookie sheets. Bake for 8 to 10 minutes.

To prepare the filling, combine all the ingredients in a large bowl. Spread a tablespoon (or more, if desired) on half of the cookies. Top with another cookie to create a sandwich.

♪ *Kids love these, an Amish tradition*

When completed in 1804, George Read II's mansion on The Strand in New Castle boasted a kitchen that was technologically advanced for its era. Years later, in the late 1820s and early 1830s, Mr. Read copied over ninety recipes for baked goods and desserts into a small notebook. Manuscript cookbooks compiled by men are rare, so this one in the collections of the Historical Society of Delaware is a real treasure.

~

George Read II's Wilmington Cake

Take 1 lb. of flour, ¾ lb. of sugar, ½ lb. of butter, a spoonful of lard, 4 eggs well beaten, mix all together with 15 drops of Essence of Lemon.

Italian Cookie Delights

Yields 4 to 5 dozen cookies

Cookies

3¾ cups flour
1 teaspoon baking powder
1 teaspoon baking soda
¼ teaspoon salt
2 sticks butter
2 cups sugar
3 eggs
2½ teaspoons pure vanilla extract
1 pound Ricotta cheese

Icing

2 cups 10x confectioners' sugar
3 tablespoons softened butter
1 teaspoon pure vanilla extract
Milk, for thinning
Colored nonpareils

Cookie dough should be placed so that the cookies are an inch or two apart when they are finished baking. When cookies are crowded, they tend to "soak" in steam from the cookies around them, making them tough or greasy. It is also important to keep the cookies from touching as they cool on a rack, so they don't become soggy.

Preheat the oven to 350°F. Combine the flour, baking powder, baking soda, and salt in a medium bowl. Cream the butter with an electric mixer, and add the sugar gradually until fully incorporated. Add the eggs one at a time, blending well after each addition. Pour in the vanilla; stir in the ricotta cheese. Add the dry mixture slowly in batches until well combined.

Drop the dough by teaspoonfuls onto an ungreased sheet. Bake 10 minutes, or until lightly golden on the bottom. Remove from the oven and cool on wire racks.

To prepare the icing, combine the confectioners' sugar, butter, and vanilla in a small bowl, stirring to a paste. Add milk, a teaspoon at the time, and continue to stir until the icing reaches the desired consistency. When completely cool, top each cooking with some of the icing and dip in the nonpareils.

Butterscotch Oatmeal Cookies

Yields 6½ dozen cookies

1 (11 ounce) package butterscotch chips
1½ cups butter
1½ cups firmly packed dark brown sugar
2 cups flour
4 cups rolled oats
2 teaspoons baking soda
4 tablespoons boiling water

Preheat the oven to 350°F. Lightly grease a cookie sheet or set aside a nonstick cookie sheet.

Place the butterscotch chips and butter in large microwave-safe bowl, and microwave on high for 1 minute. Stir, microwave on high another minute, and stir again to blend. Combine the brown sugar, flour, and oats in a medium bowl, breaking up any large lumps of brown sugar. In a small bowl, combine the baking soda with the boiling water and add to the butterscotch mixture. Add the flour mixture slowly, in batches, to the melted butterscotch with an electric mixture set on low.

Let the batter rest 5 minutes, and then drop by tablespoonfuls onto the cookie sheet. (A standard 11 x 17-inch pan should hold about 15 cookies.) Bake for 7 to 8 minutes until the cookies are firm and lightly browned around the edges. Remove from oven and let cool for 3 to 5 minutes before transferring to wire racks to finish cooling. Store in an airtight container or freeze for later use.

Happiness is a perfume you cannot pour on others without getting a few drops on yourself.

~ Ralph Waldo Emerson

For 1 square (ounce) chocolate, you can substitute 3 or 4 tablespoons cocoa plus ½ tablespoon butter or margarine.

~

Fisher's Popcorn, the well-loved caramel-corn made in Fenwick Island, has received mail orders from as far away as Vietnam and Indonesia.

Cranberry Oatmeal White Chocolate Cookies

Yields about 5 dozen cookies

⅔ cup butter, softened
⅔ cup packed light brown sugar
2 eggs
1½ cups old-fashioned rolled oats
1½ cups all-purpose flour
1 teaspoon baking soda
½ teaspoon salt
1½ cups sweetened dried cranberries, preferably Craisins
⅔ cup white chocolate chips

Preheat the oven to 375°F. Combine the butter and sugar together. Add the eggs and mix well. Combine the oats, flour, baking soda, and salt in separate bowl. Add to butter mixture in several batches, stirring well to incorporate. Stir in the Craisins and white chocolate chips. Drop by rounded teaspoonfuls onto an ungreased cookie sheet. Bake for 10 minutes, or until golden brown.

Christmas Shortbread

Yields about 4 dozen cookies

1 cup butter, at room temperature
¾ cup sifted confectioners' sugar
1 teaspoon pure vanilla extract
2 cups sifted flour
½ teaspoon salt
6 ounces semi-sweet or bittersweet chocolate
1 teaspoon vegetable shortening
Walnut or pecan halves

Preheat the oven to 300°F. Cream the butter, sugar, vanilla in a medium bowl with an electric mixer. Add the flour and salt, mixing well to incorporate. Cover and chill the dough for better handling, and then roll out to about ¼ inch thick, or thinner if you prefer. Cut out cookies using 2-inch round cookie cutters. Bake for 20 to 25 minutes, or until lightly browned around the edges. Remove the cookies to wire racks to cool. Melt the chocolate and shortening in a small saucepan on low heat. Once melted, place a teaspoonful of the chocolate mixture in the middle of each cookie. Top the chocolate with a walnut or pecan half and let cool to set.

Oatmeal Cranberry Chip Cookies

Yields 5 dozen cookies

1 cup butter-flavored shortening

1¼ cups firmly packed light brown sugar

½ cup granulated sugar

2 eggs

2 tablespoons milk

2 teaspoons pure vanilla extract

1¾ cups all-purpose flour

1 teaspoon baking soda

½ teaspoons salt

2½ cups uncooked oatmeal (quick or old fashioned)

1 cup white chocolate chips

1 cup dried cranberries

1 cup chopped pecans

Preheat the oven to 375°F. Beat together the shortening, brown sugar, and granulated sugar with an electric mixer until creamy. Add the eggs, milk, and vanilla, beating well. Add the flour, baking soda, and salt, and continue to mix well. Stir in the oats, chocolate chips, cranberries, and nuts. Mix well.

Drop by rounded tablespoonfuls onto an ungreased cookie sheet. Bake for 9 to 10 minutes, or until lightly golden. (Alternatively, press the dough into the bottom of a 9 x 13-inch baking pan for bar cookies. Bake for 30 to 35 minutes.) Remove from oven and let cool for 1 minute before transferring to wire racks to finish cooling.

Most cookie doughs (particularly drop cookies) freeze extremely well. Next time you are baking, try freezing half of your dough, tightly wrapped in a double layer of plastic. When the urge for fresh cookies hits, just thaw 20 minutes or so, then bake as usual.

Lemon Crisps

Yields about 3 dozen cookies

1 cup unsalted butter

1 cup sugar

1 egg

1½ teaspoons lemon extract

1½ cups sifted all-purpose flour

Preheat the oven to 375°F. Cream together the butter and sugar in a large bowl with an electric mixture until smooth. Add the egg, mixing on medium-high until fluffy. Stir in the lemon extract. Add the flour in batches, mixing well to fully incorporate. Drop by tablespoonfuls onto ungreased cookie sheets. Bake for 6 to 8 minutes, or until light golden. Cool on wire racks and store in an airtight container until ready to use.

Snickerdoodles

Yields about 4 dozen cookies

2 cups all-purpose flour
2 teaspoons cream of tartar
1 teaspoon baking soda
¼ teaspoon salt
2 sticks unsalted butter, softened and divided
1¾ cups sugar, divided
2 large eggs
5 teaspoons cinnamon

Preheat the oven to 350°F. Grease several cookie sheets. Sift together the flour, cream of tartar, baking soda, and salt in a medium bowl. In a separate bowl, beat together 1 cup of the unsalted butter with 1½ cups of the sugar until well blended. Add the eggs and continue beating until well incorporated. Gradually add the flour mixture to the butter mixture until well mixed and smooth. In a small bowl, combine the remaining ¼ cup of sugar with the cinnamon. Pull off pieces of the dough and roll between the palms to form generous 1¼-inch balls. Roll the balls in the cinnamon-sugar mixture. Space about 2¾ inches apart on the cookie sheets. Bake, 1 sheet at a time, in the upper third of the oven for 8 to 11 minutes, or until cookies are light golden brown around the edges. Rotate the sheets halfway through baking for even browning.

Transfer the sheet to wire racks and let stand until cookies firm up slightly, 1 to 2 minutes. Then, transfer the cookies to wire racks to cool thoroughly. Be sure to cool cookie sheets between batches or cookies may spread too much. Store the cooled cookies in an airtight container for up to 10 days or freeze for up to 1 month.

Thanks to the efforts of environmentally aware residents in Delaware and Pennsylvania, the entire White Clay Creek, which runs through both states, is now included in the National Wild and Scenic River System.

Lemon Curd Bars

Yields 18 (3 x 2-inch) bars

2 cups all-purpose flour
½ cup confectioners' sugar, plus more for dusting
¾ cup unsalted butter, chilled
6 large eggs
3 cups granulated sugar
Grated zest of 2 lemons
1 cup plus 5 tablespoons freshly squeezed lemon juice (about 5 lemons)

Preheat the oven to 325°F. Sift together 1½ cups of the flour and the confectioners' sugar in a large bowl. Cut in the butter using a pastry blender or knife until the texture is the size of small peas. Press the mixture into the bottom of a 13 x 9-inch pan and ¾ inch up the sides. Bake on the middle oven rack for 20 to 30 minutes, or until golden brown. Remove from the oven and set aside. Reduce the oven temperature to 300°F. Whisk together the eggs, lemon zest, lemon juice, and granulated sugar in a medium bowl until the eggs are smooth. Add the remaining ½ cup of flour, stirring until well combined.

Pour the batter over the baked crust. Return to the oven and bake on the middle oven rack for 35 minutes, or until set. Transfer the pan to a wire rack and let cool completely. Sprinkle with additional confectioners' sugar before cutting into bars. Store, refrigerated, in an airtight container for 2 to 3 days, or freeze for up to 1 month.

To get the most juice out of fresh lemons, bring them to room temperature and roll them under your palm against the kitchen counter before squeezing.

Colorful hot air balloons fill the skies above Sussex County during the Delmarva Hot Air Balloon Festival in Milton. Balloon teams from across the country compete in air races, while those more down to earth enjoy live entertainment, craft shows, and plenty of good food.

Banana Bars

Yields 24 bars

Bars

⅔ cup sugar
½ cup sour cream
2 tablespoons butter, softened
2 egg whites
¾ cup mashed very-ripe bananas (about 2 medium)
1 teaspoon pure vanilla extract
1 cup flour
¼ teaspoon salt
½ teaspoon baking soda
2 tablespoons finely chopped walnuts

Frosting

1¼ cups confectioners' sugar
1 tablespoon margarine, softened
1 to 2 tablespoons milk
½ teaspoon pure vanilla extract

Preheat the oven to 375°F. Spray a 9-inch square baking pan with nonstick cooking spray. Beat the sugar, sour cream, butter, and egg whites in large bowl with an electric mixer on low speed for 1 minute, scraping the bowl occasionally. Beat in the bananas and vanilla on low speed for 30 seconds. Increase the speed to medium, and add in the flour, salt, and baking powder, scraping the bowl occasionally. Stir in the nuts, and then spread the dough into the baking pan.

Bake 20 to 25 minutes, or until light brown. Remove from the oven and let cool. To prepare the frosting, combine all the ingredients in a medium bowl with an electric mixer. When the bars have cooled, spread with the frosting.

Rum Raisin Bars

Yields 24 bars

2¼ cups flour
1 teaspoon salt
1 teaspoon baking soda
¾ cup sugar
¾ cup packed light brown sugar
2 eggs
2 sticks of butter, softened
4 tablespoons rum
1 (12 ounce) bag chocolate covered raisins
4 ounces chocolate chips
1½ cups walnuts

Preheat the oven to 375°F. Grease a 9 x 13-inch pan. Combine the flour, salt, and baking soda in a large bowl. Add the sugar, brown sugar, eggs, and butter, and combine well with an electric mixer. Add the rum, stirring to incorporate. Gradually add the chocolate covered raisins, chocolate chips, and nuts. Spread into the pan and bake for 15 to 20 minutes. (The center should be soft but cooked.) Remove from the oven and let cool. Cut into bars and store in an airtight container until ready to serve.

♪ *This is an easy and quick recipe. Good as a cookie or warmed and served with vanilla ice cream.*

Oatmeal Fudgies

Yields 24 bars

1 cup oatmeal
¾ cup packed light brown sugar
¼ teaspoon salt
1 cup flour
½ teaspoon baking soda
¾ cup melted butter or margarine
8 ounces semi-sweet chocolate chips, or more if desired

Preheat the oven to 350°F. Grease a 9-inch square pan. Combine the oatmeal, brown sugar, salt, flour, and baking soda. Stir in the melted butter. Press half of the mixture into the bottom of the baking pan. Bake for 10 minutes. Remove from the oven and sprinkle with the chocolate chips. Sprinkle with the remainder of the oatmeal mixture and bake 15 to 20 minutes until golden brown.

When it's time to change your point of view, remember: STRESSED is just DESSERTS spelled backwards!

~

The Delaware Toy and Miniature Museum in Wilmington contains what might be the world's largest collection of miniature vases, some dating back to 600 B.C.

Unbaked Apple Balls
Yields 4 dozen

1 cup applesauce or apple butter
¾ cup granulated sugar
¾ cup packed light brown sugar
⅓ cup butter
¼ cup cocoa
3 cups uncooked oatmeal
½ teaspoon pure vanilla extract
1 cup chocolate chips, chopped pecans, walnuts, or combination
Confectioners' sugar for dusting

Line a cookie sheet with wax paper. Combine the applesauce, granulated sugar, brown sugar, butter, and cocoa in medium saucepan over medium-high heat. Bring to a boil, and let boil 5 minutes, stirring continuously until thickened. Remove from the heat, and stir in the oatmeal and vanilla. Allow to cool, and then stir in the chocolate chips. Drop by teaspoonfuls onto the cookie sheets. Roll each drop into a ball, and then roll in confectioners' sugar. Allow to dry on the cookie sheet, and then store in an airtight container until ready to serve.

To achieve a "gourmet dessert" look, fill squeeze bottles with chocolate, raspberry, caramel or any other sweet sauce, and drizzle a quick pattern across individual plates as a colorful backdrop to your dessert. If you don't have a squeeze bottle handy, just cut a tiny corner off of a ziplock bag and use that instead.

Tandy Cakes
Yields 36 bars

2 cups flour
1 teaspoon pure vanilla extract
2 cups sugar
½ teaspoon salt
1 teaspoon baking powder
1 tablespoon oil
1 cup milk
4 eggs, beaten until foamy
2 cups peanut butter
2 cups milk chocolate chips, melted

Preheat the oven to 350°F. Grease and flour a 11 x 15-inch baking sheet. Combine the flour, vanilla, sugar, salt, baking powder, oil, and milk in a large bowl. Stir in the beaten eggs. Pour the batter in a baking sheet and bake for 20 minutes. Remove from the oven and let cool. When cool, spread with the peanut butter and top with the melted chocolate. Chill in the refrigerator until set, and then cut into bars to serve.

Bayou Brownies

Yields 36 servings

3 eggs, divided
1 box yellow cake mix
1 cup coarsely chopped pecans
1 stick butter, melted
1 (8 ounce) package cream cheese
1 (16 ounce) box confectioners' sugar

Preheat the oven to 325°F. and grease a 9 x 13-inch pan. Beat 1 egg in a small bowl. Combine the cake mix, pecans, melted butter, and beaten egg together by hand. Press into the bottom of the baking pan. Beat the remaining 2 eggs until fluffy. Combine the cream cheese, confectioners' sugar, and eggs with an electric mixer. Pour over the cake-mix mixture and bake for 40 to 50 minutes, or until browned and firm to the touch. Do not undercook the brownies, or the topping will be runny.

Try using unflavored dry breadcrumbs instead of flour to coat your greased baking pans. Cakes release much more easily, and the bottom won't get soggy.

Deep Dish
Homemade Brownies

Yields 16 brownies

¾ cup butter, melted
1½ cups sugar
1½ teaspoons pure vanilla extract
3 eggs
¾ cup all-purpose flour
½ cup cocoa
½ teaspoon baking powder
½ teaspoon salt
1 cup chocolate chips

Preheat the oven to 350°F. Grease an 8-inch square pan. Combine the sugar, baking powder, salt, and chocolate chips in a medium bowl. Combine the butter, vanilla, and eggs in another bowl, mixing well to combine. Stir the butter mixture into the sugar mixture, blending well. Bake for 40 to 45 minutes, or until golden brown. Allow to cool completely, and then store in an airtight container until ready to serve.

*Never eat more than
you can lift.
~ Miss Piggy*

Kahlúa Brownies
with Butter Cream Frosting
and Chocolate Glaze

Yields 24 brownies

Crust

5⅓ tablespoons unsalted butter, room temperature
⅓ cup firmly packed light brown sugar
⅔ cup all-purpose flour, sifted
½ cup finely chopped pecans

Filling

2 ounces unsweetened chocolate
¼ cup vegetable shortening
4 tablespoons unsalted butter
2 large eggs
½ cup granulated sugar
½ cup firmly packed light brown sugar
1 teaspoon pure vanilla extract
¼ cup Kahlúa
½ cup all-purpose flour, sifted
¼ teaspoon salt
½ cup chopped pecans

Butter Cream Frosting

6 tablespoons unsalted butter, room temperature
2 cups sifted confectioners' sugar
1 tablespoon Kahlúa, or more if needed
1 tablespoon heavy whipping cream

Glaze

2 ounces semi-sweet chocolate
1 ounce unsweetened chocolate
2 teaspoons vegetable shortening

Preheat the oven to 350°F. Grease and flour a 9-inch square baking pan. To prepare the crust, cream the butter and sugar together with an electric mixer until fluffy. Slowly add the flour, mixing well. Add the pecans, stirring until well incorporated. Press the crust into the bottom of the prepared pan.

Kahlúa Brownies with Butter Cream Frosting and Chocolate Glaze, continued

To prepare the filling, combine the chocolate, shortening, and butter in a small saucepan over low heat. Stir until the chocolate is melted and the mixture is smooth. Remove from the heat and let cool. Combine the eggs, granulated sugar, brown sugar, and vanilla in a large bowl. Mix until blended. Stir into the cooled chocolate mixture. Add the Kahlúa. Slowly add the flour and salt, mixing until batter is smooth. Stir in the pecans. Pour the filling into the prepared crust. Bake 25 minutes, or until a knife inserted in the center comes out clean. Be careful not to overbake. Remove from the oven and let cool.

To prepare the frosting, cream the butter, confectioners' sugar, Kahlúa, and cream in a small bowl until smooth and creamy. Spread over the cooled filling mixture and refrigerate for 30 minutes. (Add more Kahlúa if needed to make spreading easier.) For a less sweet brownie, use only half of the frosting.

To prepare the glaze, melt the semi-sweet chocolate, unsweetened chocolate, and vegetable shortening over low heat, stirring constantly. Cool and spread over the frosting.

In the conservatories at Longwood Gardens, 4,500 types of plants thrive in 20 gardens, set within four acres under glass. Each year between January and April, 50,000 bulbs bloom inside, offering visitors an early taste of spring.

Chocolate Kahlúa Trifle

Serves 10 to 12

1 box devil's food cake mix or 9 x 13-inch store-bought cake
8 ounces Kahlúa
1 (4.6 ounce) box chocolate pudding or 2 cups pudding
1 (8 to 12 ounce) container whipped topping
5 toffee candy bars, such as Heath, Skor, Sweet Escapes, crushed

Bake the cake according to package direction and let cool. Prepare the pudding according to package directions. Break the cake into a mixing bowl. Pour in the Kahlúa and mix with a wooden spoon to a mud-like consistency. Pat the mixture into the bottom of trifle bowl. Layer the pudding over the cake mixture. Frost with the whipped topping, and sprinkle with the crushed candy bars. Chill until ready to serve.

♪ *Easy, delicious, and pretty*

Hollow out lemons and oranges to make colorful serving dishes for sherbets. Garnish with fresh mint leaves.

~

Stuff a miniature marshmallow in the bottom of a sugar cone to prevent ice cream drips.

Holiday Fudge
Serves 36

3 cups semi-sweet chocolate chips
1 (14 ounce) can sweetened condensed milk
¼ cup butter
1 cup coarsely chopped walnuts

Place the chocolate chips, condensed milk, and butter in a large, microwave-safe bowl. Microwave on medium (50%) power, stirring occasionally, until the chocolate and butter are melted. Stir in the nuts and pour into an 8-inch square baking dish lined with wax paper. Refrigerate until set. Cut into 1-inch squares and store in an airtight container.

Chocolate Orange Chip Ice Cream
Yields ½ gallon

1 tablespoon orange zest
1 cup sugar
⅛ teaspoon salt
1 pint heavy whipping cream
1 pint light cream
1 teaspoon pure vanilla extract
½ cup chocolate sauce
½ cup miniature semi-sweet chocolate chips
Ice cubes, for ice cream maker
Rock salt, for ice cream maker

Combine the orange zest, sugar, and salt in the mixing canister. Add the heavy cream and light cream. Stir in the vanilla and chocolate sauce, blending well.

Start the ice cream maker, following manufacturer's instructions for adding ice and salt to freeze. After 10 minutes of running, slowly add the chocolate chips to the canister. Let the machine continue to run until the mixture has thickened and filled the canister, about 50 minutes. Remove the canister from the ice cream maker and stir thoroughly to evenly distribute the chocolate chips and orange zest. Place in the freezer for at least 3 hours before serving.

Peppermint Bark
Yields about 24 pieces of candy

2 pounds white chocolate
12 candy canes, crushed
½ teaspoon peppermint oil

Melt the chocolate in a double boiler over medium heat. Stir in the crushed candy canes and peppermint oil. Spread onto a parchment paper-lined cookie sheet and store in the refrigerator to harden. Break the hardened bark into pieces and store, refrigerated, in an airtight container for up to 1 week.

Crisp Sugared Pecans
Yields 2½ cups of nuts

2½ cups pecan halves
1 cup sugar
½ cup water
1 teaspoon cinnamon
1 teaspoon salt
1½ teaspoons pure vanilla extract

Lightly grease a large sheet of wax paper. Lightly toast the pecan halves. Combine the sugar, water, cinnamon, and salt in a small saucepan over medium heat until the temperature reaches 236°F., or the soft-ball stage. Do not stir while cooking. (To test for the correct degree of doneness, immerse a drop of boiling liquid in cold water. If it forms a soft ball that flattens when removed, it is ready.) Remove the mixture from the heat, and gently stir in the vanilla and nuts until the nuts are well coated and the mixture becomes creamy. Turn the mixture out onto lightly greased wax paper, separating the pecan halves as they cool. Store in an airtight container until ready to serve.

♪ *This is a nice holiday snack or no stress gift,*
packaged in a decorated box or tin.

Refrigerate shelled nuts in a tightly closed container or plastic bag to keep them fresh for several months. For longer storage, freeze shelled or unshelled nuts in a tightly closed container for up to one year.

~

Delaware's state tree is the American Holly, thanks to the town of Milton's once thriving business of providing holly wreaths to the nation.

Chocolate Mousse Cake

Serves 8 to 12

30 Oreo cookies

6 tablespoons unsalted butter, room temperature

12 ounces semisweet chocolate chips

1 teaspoon pure vanilla extract

½ teaspoon peppermint extract or 1 teaspoon almond extract (optional)

3 cups heavy whipping cream, chilled and divided

¼ cup sugar

1 good-quality chocolate bar with or without almonds, room temperature, for garnish

Preheat the oven to 350°F. Butter a 9-inch springform pan. Finely grind the cookies in a food processor. Add the butter and process until evenly moist. Remove from the food processor and press into the bottom and up the sides of the pan. Bake for 5 minutes, then set aside to cool.

Wipe the crumbs from the processor bowl, and add the chocolate chips and vanilla. Add the peppermint or almond extract, if desired. Process until the chips are finely ground.

Bring 1 cup of the cream just to boil in a small saucepan over medium-high heat. With the processor running, gradually add the hot cream, processing until smooth. Transfer the chocolate mixture to large bowl and let cool.

Once the mixture has cooled, beat the remaining 2 cups of cream with the sugar in large bowl to stiff peaks. Gently fold into the chocolate mixture, just until the color is uniform throughout. Pour the chocolate filling into the crust and refrigerate until set, about 6 hours. To garnish the cake, run a vegetable peeler along the long edge of the chocolate bar to create chocolate shavings. Garnish with the shavings, and keep refrigerated until ready to serve. (The cake can be made up to 1 day ahead.)

♪ *This simple, yet elegant dessert never fails to get rave reviews.*

For the prettiest chocolate shavings, bring white or milk chocolate to room temperature, and shave with a vegetable peeler.

Crazy Cake
Serves 10 to 12

1½ cups flour
1 cup sugar
½ teaspoon salt
1 teaspoon baking soda
3 heaping tablespoons cocoa
1 teaspoon pure vanilla extract
1 tablespoon vinegar
⅓ cup oil
1 cup water or coffee

Preheat the oven to 375°F. Sift the flour, sugar, salt, baking soda, and cocoa into a 9 x 13-inch rectangular cake pan. Smooth the ingredients out with a fork. Make 3 holes in the mixture. In one hole, pour the vanilla. In the next, pour the vinegar, and in the third, pour the oil. Pour the water over all the mixture, and beat with a fork until smooth. Bake for 25 minutes, or until a knife inserted in the center comes out clean.

If you bake your cakes in nonstick pans, turn your oven down 25 degrees Fahrenheit, and check for doneness about five minutes earlier than usual.

Raw Apple Cake
Serves 12

3 cups flour, sifted
2 cups sugar
1 tablespoon cinnamon
1 teaspoon salt
1 teaspoon baking soda
Nutmeg to taste
½ cup nuts (optional)
1½ cups oil
2 eggs, slightly beaten
1 tablespoon pure vanilla extract
3 cups peeled and sliced McIntosh apples (3 or 4 apples)

Preheat the oven to 325°F. Grease a 9 x 13-inch baking pan. Combine the flour, sugar, cinnamon, salt, baking soda, nutmeg, and nuts in a large bowl. Add the oil, eggs, and vanilla; mix well. Gently stir in the apple slices. Bake for 1 hour, or until a knife inserted in the center comes out clean.

Orange Poppy Seed Cake
Serves 10 to 12

Cinnamon sugar, for dusting
1 cup fat-free sour cream
3 eggs or ¾ cup egg beaters
1 yellow cake mix
1 (6 ounce) can frozen orange juice concentrate, thawed
1 to 2 tablespoons poppy seeds

Preheat the oven to 350°F. Spray a Bundt pan with cooking spray and dust with cinnamon sugar. Combine the sour cream, eggs, and cake mix in a large bowl. Add the orange juice and poppy seed, stirring well to incorporate. Pour the batter into the prepared Bundt pan and bake about 45 minutes, or until a knife inserted in the center comes out clean.

To decorate a dessert plate, place a large doily in the center of the plate and dust with cocoa (for white plates) or powdered sugar (for colored plates).

Raspberry Torte
Serves 12

1¼ cups flour
1¼ cups sugar, divided
¼ teaspoon salt
2 sticks butter, chilled
3 tablespoons cornstarch
1 cup sugar
2 (10 ounce) packages frozen red raspberries, thawed
2 cups whipped cream

Preheat the oven to 350°F. To prepare the crust, combine the flour, ¼ cup of the sugar, and the salt. Cut in the chilled butter with a pastry blender until the mixture resembles coarse crumbs. Pat the crust into the bottom of a 13 x 9 x 2-inch pan. Bake for 15 to 18 minutes, or until lightly browned. Remove from the oven and let cool.

To prepare the filling, combine the cornstarch with the remaining cup of sugar in a medium saucepan. Add the raspberries and cook, stirring constantly until the mixture comes to a boil and thickens. Cool slightly, and then pour over the cooled crust.

Refrigerate about 3 hours to chill. Top with whipped cream when ready to serve.

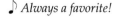 *Always a favorite!*

Lemon Pecan Pound Cake

Serves 8 to 10

Cake

1 cup butter, softened
2 cups confectioners' sugar
3 eggs
1⅓ cups all-purpose flour
1 teaspoon pure vanilla extract
½ cup chopped pecans
1 tablespoon grated lemon zest

Glaze

3 tablespoons freshly squeezed lemon juice
⅓ cup sugar

Preheat the oven to 325°F. Grease an 8-inch square foil pan. Cream the butter and sugar in a large bowl with an electric mixer until fluffy. Add the eggs one at a time, beating well after each addition. Stir in the flour and vanilla. Continue beating until just mixed. Fold in the pecans and lemon zest. Pour the batter into the pan. Bake for 50 minutes, or until a knife inserted in the center comes out clean. Remove to wire rack to cool. While the cake is still hot, combine the lemon juice and sugar to make the glaze. Brush liberally over the warm cake.

Known for their rich taste and moist texture, pound cakes were originally named for the pound each of butter, sugar, eggs and flour used to make them. The secret to making a moist cake that is not too heavy is to let the eggs come to room temperature before adding them to the batter. This results in a greater volume of batter and thus, a higher, lighter cake.

~

Icing on the Cake

Face it: There's never enough icing to go around. Just for fun, start with one round 8 or 9-inch cake, and cut it into wedges. Separate wedges and place them on a wire rack, then ladle on your icing of choice. Transfer each slice to a plate, and for a special occasion, add a festive decoration, like sugared edible violets. Your guests will be thrilled!

Lemon Cake

Serves 10 to 12

Cake

3 cups flour
2 teaspoons baking soda
½ teaspoon salt
½ pound butter, softened
2 cups sugar
4 large eggs
1 cup milk
2 tablespoons grated lemon zest

Glaze

¾ cup sugar
⅓ cup freshly squeezed lemon juice

Preheat the oven to 325°F. Grease and flour a tube pan. Sift together the flour, baking soda, and salt. Cream the butter and sugar together with an electric mixer in a medium bowl until light. Add the eggs one at a time, mixing thoroughly after each one. Add the lemon zest. Fold in the sifted flour mixture in batches, alternating with the milk until blended. Pour into the prepared tube pan. Bake for 1 hour and 15 minutes, or until a knife inserted in the center comes out clean.

While the cake is baking, combine the sugar and lemon juice for a glaze. After the cake is removed from the oven, cool slightly, and then remove from pan. Pour the glaze over the top and sides of cake until all the glaze is absorbed. Garnish with fresh raspberries, strawberries, or blueberries and top with whipped cream for a real indulgence.

To add an elegant finishing touch to desserts, garnish with a fruit coulis. To make a coulis, puree fruit such as raspberries or strawberries with a small amount of sugar or honey, and if you like, some brandy. Strain out any seeds by pouring through a sieve. Then dip a spoon into the coulis and drizzle designs on the plate. Top your dessert with a small amount of fresh fruit (for instance, whole raspberries or sliced strawberries) and perhaps a sprig of fresh mint, for a professional looking presentation.

~

Don't omit the salt from your cake recipes. A small amount of salt heightens the perception of sweetness, and enhances the flavor of your cake.

Chocolate Truffle Loaf
with Raspberry Sauce
Serves 12

Truffle Loaf

2 cups heavy cream, divided

3 egg yolks, slightly beaten

2 (8 ounce) packages semi-sweet chocolate

½ cup light corn syrup

½ cup butter

¼ cup confectioners' sugar

1 teaspoon pure vanilla extract

Raspberry Sauce

1 (10 ounce) package frozen raspberries, thawed

⅓ cup light corn syrup

Line an 8¼ x 4½ x 2½-loaf pan (or 2 smaller loaf pans) with plastic wrap. Combine ½ cup of the cream with the egg yolks in a small bowl. Combine the chocolate, corn syrup, and butter in a 3-quart saucepan over medium heat, stirring until melted. Add the egg mixture and cook 3 minutes, stirring constantly. Remove from the heat and cool to room temperature.

Combine the remaining 1½ cups of cream, the sugar, and vanilla in a large bowl. Beat until soft peaks form. Fold the whipped cream into the chocolate until no streaks remain. Pour into the loaf pan and refrigerate overnight.

To prepare the sauce, purée the raspberries in a blender, and then pour in the corn syrup, pulsing lightly to combine. Pour the raspberry mixture through a fine sieve to strain all the seeds from the sauce.

To serve the truffle, slice the loaf into ¾-inch slices. Drizzle the raspberry sauce on individual serving plates and place a slice of chocolate truffle on top.

In need of a pastry bag? For a quick and easy substitute, cut a tiny corner off of a ziplock bag. Fill with icing, whipped cream, or coulis, seal the bag, and squeeze gently.

~

Protecting Berries

Ripe berries are so tender they burst in your mouth ~ if they don't get squashed in the carton first. Dessert chefs have a secret for keeping them intact: As soon as you get home from the store, scatter them gently on a baking sheet lined with several layers of paper towels, then store in the refrigerator until you're ready to wash and eat them.

Blueberry Upside Down Cake

Serves 9

Cake

1½ cups flour
¼ teaspoon salt
½ teaspoon baking soda
½ teaspoon cinnamon
½ teaspoon allspice
¾ teaspoon ground ginger
½ cup butter, softened
½ cup sugar
1 egg
½ cup molasses
½ cup plus 2 tablespoons buttermilk

Topping

2 tablespoons butter, softened
¼ cup sugar
Zest of 1 lemon
2 tablespoons light corn syrup
2 cups blueberries

Although buttermilk has a refrigerator shelf life of up to three weeks, it tends to separate, so shake the container before each use.

Sift together the flour, salt, baking soda, cinnamon, allspice, and ginger in a medium bowl. Cream the butter and sugar together in a medium bowl with an electric mixer. Add the egg, beating well. Stir in the molasses. Add the flour mixture in batches, alternating with the buttermilk, until well combined.

For the topping, combine the butter, sugar, lemon zest, and corn syrup in an 8-inch square pan. Gently stir in the blueberries. Pour the batter over the berries and bake at 325 for about 1 hour. Remove from the oven and turn upside down over a serving plate. Allow to sit until all the topping comes out of the pan. Serve warm with whipped cream or ice cream.

Mini and Moist Chocolate Cakes with Fudge Sauce

Serves 6

Sauce

4½ ounces bittersweet or semisweet chocolate, chopped
2 ounces unsweetened chocolate, chopped
⅓ cup hot water
¼ cup light corn syrup

Cake

5 ounces bittersweet or semisweet chocolate, chopped
10 tablespoons (1¼ sticks) unsalted butter
3 large eggs
3 large egg yolks
1½ cups confectioners' sugar
½ cup all-purpose flour
Vanilla ice cream, for topping

To prepare the sauce, combine both chocolates in the top of a double boiler over barely simmering water, stirring occasionally until melted. Add the hot water and corn syrup, and whisk until smooth. Remove the top pan from the double boiler and let cool slightly. (The sauce can be made up to 2 days ahead. Cover well and store in the refrigerator. Before serving, rewarm in a saucepan over low heat, stirring constantly.)

To prepare the cake, preheat the oven to 450°F. Butter six ¾-cup soufflé dishes or custard cups. Combine the chocolate and butter in heavy medium saucepan over low heat, stirring until melted. Remove from the heat to let cool slightly. Whisk the eggs and egg yolks in large bowl, until well blended. Whisk in the sugar, and then whisk in the chocolate mixture. Whisk in the flour until well combined. Pour the batter into dishes, dividing equally. (The cakes can be made up to this point 1 day ahead. Cover and refrigerate until ready to bake.)

Bake the cakes until the sides are set, but the center remains soft and runny, about 11 minutes (or up to 14 minutes for batter that has been refrigerated). Run a small knife around each cake to loosen from the dishes. Immediately turn the cakes out onto serving plates. Spoon the warmed sauce around the cakes and serve with vanilla ice cream.

♪ *These cakes are slightly underbaked so the chocolate center oozes when they are eaten.*

To make cakes easier to serve, sprinkle the cake platter with sugar before laying down the bottom layer.

~

Too much of a good thing can be wonderful.
~ Mae West

Luscious Chocolate Cheesecake

Serves 10 to 12

Cake

⅓ cup melted margarine or butter
1¼ cups graham cracker crumbs
¼ cup sugar
3 (8 ounce) packages cream cheese softened
1 (14 ounce) can sweetened condensed milk
1 (12 ounce) package semi-sweet chocolate chips
4 eggs
2 teaspoons pure vanilla extract

Unwrap packages of cream cheese, butter or margarine before bringing them to room temperature; it is easier than scraping them off the foil.

Sauce

1 (20 ounce) can raspberry pie filling
Splash of framboise

Preheat the oven to 300°F. Combine the margarine, graham cracker crumbs, and sugar. Pat the mixture firmly into the bottom of a 9-inch springform pan. Beat the cream cheese with an electric mixer until fluffy. Add the sweetened condensed milk, and beat until smooth. Melt the chocolate chips in the microwave on high, stirring occasionally. Add the melted chocolate to the cream cheese mixture. Beat in the eggs and vanilla, blending thoroughly to combine. Pour the filling over the crust in the pan. Bake 1 hour and 5 minutes, or until the cake springs back when lightly touched. Cool to room temperature, and then chill in the refrigerator. Remove the side of the pan, and transfer the cheesecake to a serving platter.

To prepare the sauce, combine the pie filling with a splash of framboise in a microwave-safe bowl. Heat the sauce in the microwave, and then pour over the cheesecake.

♪ *Always enjoyed by chocolate lovers.*

Bavarian Apple Torte

Serves 10 to 12

Pastry

½ cup margarine
⅓ cup sugar
¼ teaspoon pure vanilla extract
1 cup flour

Filling

1 (8 ounce) package cream cheese, room temperature
¼ cup sugar
1 egg
½ teaspoon pure vanilla extract

Apple Topping

4 cups peeled and thinly sliced cooking apples
⅓ cup sugar
½ teaspoon cinnamon
¼ cup sliced almonds

Preheat the oven to 450°F. To prepare the pastry, cream the margarine and sugar together with an electric mixture until fluffy. Blend in the vanilla; add the flour and mix well. Press the dough into the bottom and 1½ inches up the sides of a 9 or 10-inch springform pan.

For the filling, combine the cream cheese and sugar until well blended. Beat in the egg and vanilla, mixing well. Pour over the dough in the springform pan.

For the topping, toss the sliced apples with the sugar and cinnamon. Layer over the cream cheese in a circular pattern. Sprinkle with almonds and bake for 10 minutes. Reduce the temperature to 375°F. and bake for 25 more minutes. Remove from the oven and loosen the cake from rim of pan with a knife or spatula. Chill until ready to serve.

In 1785, Oliver Evans of Newport, Delaware, invented the automatic flour-milling machinery that revolutionized the industry.

Where can you find not only bands and tailgating, but giant catapults hurling pumpkins across a field? At the annual World Championship Punkin Chunkin' Competition in Lewes, Delaware, of course! In 1986, one medievally minded friend challenged another to see who could catapult a pumpkin the farthest. Before long, the field of two had grown thirty-fold, attracting participants from as far away as Illinois, Texas, Maine and Florida. The Punkin Chunkin' has gotten national media coverage, and even grabbed the attention of David Letterman!

Punkin Chunkin' Cinnamon Meringues

Yield 10 to 15 shells

Meringues

3 egg whites, room temperature
¼ teaspoon cream of tartar
¼ teaspoon pure vanilla extract
¼ teaspoon almond extract
½ teaspoon ground cinnamon
⅛ teaspoon salt
½ cup sugar

Filling

1 (3 ounce) package vanilla flavored cook-and-serve pudding
2 cups reduced-fat (2%) milk
½ cup fresh or canned pumpkin
¼ teaspoon almond extract
⅛ teaspoon fresh grated nutmeg
⅓ cup finely chopped pecans, for garnish
Whipped cream, for garnish
Green cherries, for garnish

To prepare the meringue shells, preheat the oven to 250°F. Line a baking sheet with parchment paper. Beat the egg whites in a large bowl with an electric mixer on high until foamy. Sprinkle in the cream of tartar, vanilla extract, almond extract, cinnamon, and salt. Continue beating until soft peaks form. Gradually add the sugar, 1 tablespoon at a time, beating until stiff peaks form. Do not underbeat.

Drop the meringues onto the baking sheet, ¼ cupful at a time. Shape into circles and build up the sides to create meringue "cups." Bake for 1 hour. Turn off the oven and, keeping the oven door shut, leave the meringues in the oven for an additional 1½ hours. Remove from the oven and allow to cool at room temperature.

To prepare the pumpkin filling, combine the pudding mix and milk in a medium saucepan. Set over medium heat and stir in the pumpkin, almond extract, and nutmeg, stirring continuously until

Punkin Chunkin' Cinnamon Meringues, continued

the mixture comes to a boil. Remove from the heat and transfer to a separate bowl. Cover with plastic wrap and refrigerate. When well chilled, fill the meringue cups with the pudding. Sprinkle with the pecans, dot with whipped cream, and top with a green cherry.

♪ *This recipe won a prize at the annual Pumpkin Chunk Recipe contest in 1997.*

Grasshopper Pie

Serves 8

4 tablespoons butter, melted
18 Hydrox cookies, crushed
25 marshmallows
½ cup milk
4 tablespoons green crème de menthe
2 tablespoons white crème de cacao
1 cup whipped cream

Combine the melted butter with the crushed cookies in a small bowl. Press into a 9-inch pie pan for the crust. Combine the marshmallows and milk in a double boiler, stirring occasionally until melted. Transfer the marshmallow mixture to a medium bowl, cover, and refrigerate until slightly chilled, about 1 hour. Stir in the crème de menthe and crème de cacao. Fold in the whipped cream. Pour the mixture into the pie shell and freeze. About two hours before serving, transfer the pie to the refrigerator to allow it to soften slightly before slicing.

The annual Punkin Chunkin' is held on the first Saturday after Halloween, in Lewes, Delaware. The contestants' goal is to make a pumpkin fly as far as possible, using a variety of creative mechanical means. While the object is to make the longest "chunk," any improvement of a personal best is cause for celebration.

"Chunkers" support many nonprofit organizations that help stage this event, and also present scholarships for higher education in the fields of Engineering, Agriculture, Mechanical Technology and Sciences.

Classic Vanilla Crème Brûlée

Serves 6

3 cups heavy cream
¼ cup granulated sugar
3 whole eggs
5 egg yolks
1 teaspoon pure vanilla extract
Vanilla from 2 vanilla beans
Granulated sugar, for topping

Preheat the oven to 300°F. Heat the cream and sugar in a heavy saucepan until almost boiling. Combine the whole eggs and egg yolks in a medium bowl, beating well. Gradually pour the heated cream into the eggs, whisking continuously to avoid curdling, and then return to the mixture to the saucepan. Cook over moderate heat, stirring constantly with a wooden spoon, until the custard coats the back of the spoon, about 3 to 4 minutes. Remove from the heat and stir in the vanilla extract and vanilla beans.

Pour the custard into six individual custard dishes or into a single, shallow 9-inch baking dish. Set the ramekins or baking dish in a large pan and place on the middle rack of the oven. Pour hot water into the outer pan to come level with custard for a water bath. Bake for 35 to 40 minutes, or until center of the custard is set. When cooked, remove the custard from water bath and let cool. Cover and chill. A few hours before serving, preheat the broiler. Sift the sugar evenly over the top of custard, spreading to the edges. Set the custard under broiler as close to the heat as possible. Broil until browned but not burned, about 1½ minutes. Watch closely. Alternatively, use a kitchen torch to brown the sugar. Chill and serve.

What is the difference between crème brûlée, flan and crème caramel? They are all baked custard desserts, but the caramel coating and the texture of the custard vary. Crème brûlée is a French dessert with a brittle sugar topping over creamy custard. The caramel for flan and crème caramel (from Spain and France, respectively), is first poured into molds, then topped with custard. After the custard has baked and set, the mold is inverted onto a serving dish and the caramel syrup forms a sauce rather than a crust. The custard is usually firmer, with a more egg-like flavor than that of crème brûlée.

~

Sweets to the sweet: farewell!
~ Hamlet, V, i, 265

Decorating with Sauces

Decorating plates with sauces adds both color and drama, and can be done for entrées and desserts. For a pretty presentation, try one of the following:

~ A single sauce, pooled center or off-center on the plate, especially if it is a bold color.

~ One or more colored sauces, drizzled or splattered onto the plate for an artistic effect. Lightly dip a pastry brush in sauce, then run your thumb over the tips of the bristles, letting the sauce splatter onto the plate.

~ For a more defined pattern, apply sauce(s) using squirt bottles. This technique works best with cold sauces such as vanilla, caramel, chocolate or fruit coulis. The sauce must be thick enough to hold the pattern created, and if more than one sauce is used, they should all be of the same viscosity. The empty plate may be decorated first, or the sauce can be applied with the dessert in place.

In 1990, internationally known Andrew Wyeth, a resident of Chadds Ford, Pennsylvania, became the first artist to be honored with The Congressional Gold Medal.

Patterns to Try

~ Using two sauces, pool the first evenly across an empty plate, and create a spiral on top of it with the second. Draw a thin-bladed knife or toothpick through the sauces from the center point to just inside the edge, then move over an inch or two (depending on the size of your plate) and carefully pull back from the edge to the center. Continue rotating around the plate, spacing your lines as evenly as possible. The result is a spider web effect; place your dessert in the center.

~ Apply 2 sauces to an empty plate in parallel lines, alternating colors. There should be no space between the lines. Carefully pull a toothpick from top to bottom, then from bottom to top of the plate, continuing to alternate perpendicular to the parallel lines. This is especially pretty when done over half of the plate, with the dessert placed slightly off-center so that it overlaps both the design and the empty portion of the plate.

~ Squirt a light colored sauce evenly around the edge of the plate (creating a rim inside the rim). Evenly space dots of a darker sauce on top, then gently pull a toothpick through the sauces, going once around the entire circumference of the plate. This creates a wreath of hearts or leaves, depending on the size of the dots.

Notes

**Above: Delaware
Coastline**

**Right: Delaware
Bay**

Promenade
Menus

Delaware Seashore State Park

With a coastline 28 miles long, Delaware has a lot to offer beach-goers. From Cape Henlopen south to Fenwick Island, you can find many areas of picturesque seclusion, allowing you to feast your eyes on the beauty of the dunes and the Atlantic. Then again, you might prefer the exciting nightlife at Dewey Beach. Or perhaps you'd like to relax with your family at Bethany. Or, as many visitors have discovered, there's always lots to do on the Boardwalk in Rehoboth, whose proximity to Washington, D.C. has earned it the nickname, "The Nation's Summer Capital." Whatever you choose, you're sure to find it in Delaware.

Photograph by Kevin Fleming,
courtesy of the Delaware Tourism Office,
Delaware Economic Development Office

Delaware Bay

The beaches along the Delaware Bay beckon with their own recipe for relaxation. Whether you enjoy fishing, bird watching, swimming, boating, a good book or a walk along an uncrowded beach, you'll find it here. Many of these beaches also offer a special attraction: You can watch the sun rise over the bay, and beautiful sunsets over the marsh. And, of course, you can always enjoy a picnic, a campfire, or dining by candlelight.

Photograph by Patsy Keller

Eight at 8:00

Brie with Bourbon p. 18

Tapenade p. 11

Fresh Fig, Gorgonzola and Walnut Salad p. 72

Stuffed Beef Tenderloin p. 128

Fresh Asparagus Risotto p. 162

Brussels Sprouts in Pecan Butter p. 159

Classic Vanilla Crème Brûlée p. 206

One can never pay in gratitude; one can only pay "in kind" somewhere else in life.

~ Anne Morrow Lindbergh

Comfort For A Friend

Potato Soup p. 56

Curried Chicken Curl Ups p. 120

Spinach and Rice p. 165

The Ultimate Chocolate Chip Cookies p. 178

Friendship Tea p. 37

Henry Ford invented both the Model T and the charcoal briquette. Little did he know he was helping to invent tailgating!

Blue Hen Brunch

Three-Way Strawberry-Spinach Salad p. 79

Macadamia Nut French Toast p. 47

Asparagus Egg Bake with Mornay Sauce p. 50

Bedeviled Bacon p. 51

Pineapple Casserole p. 171

Touchdown Tailgate - A Sporting Event

Chicken Chutney Spread p. 14

Hoagie Dip p. 13

Authentic Buffalo Wings p. 29

Chili For A Crowd p. 67

Beer Bread p. 41

Deep Dish Homemade Brownies p. 189

Meet Me By The Brandywine

Smoky White Bean Dip p. 11

Bourbon Barbequed Ribs p. 143

Hoisin Chicken Skewers p. 116

Citrus Couscous Salad p. 74

Black Bean and Rice Salad p. 72

Chocolate Orange Chip Ice Cream p. 192

❧

Bethany Beach Buffet

Delaware Crab Delight p. 19

Marinated Shrimp p. 23

Lobster Stew p. 64

Grilled Clam Bake p. 102

Summer Vegetable Rice Pilaf p. 166

Roasted Corn, Black Bean, and Mango Salad p. 73

Blueberry Upside Down Cake p. 200

Sangría Blanca p. 39

Candlelight may be romantic, but there's nothing lovely about scraping melted candles out of their holders. Not only is it difficult, you also risk scratching or breaking the often delicate glass. Instead, place the votive holders in the freezer for a few hours; the wax should shrink just enough to pop right out. This trick also works to remove wax from a candlestick.

A Quick Fix for Tarnished Silver

Put your silver or silver plate one or two pieces deep into an aluminum pan, or in a laundry tub lined with several pieces of aluminum foil. Sprinkle ¼ to ½ cup baking soda over your silver, then cover with boiling water. Let sit until it stops bubbling, then rinse and buff dry with a soft cloth. Repeat for heavily tarnished silver.

Diamond Cocktail Party

Feta Shrimp Triangles p. 24

Hot Onion Soufflé p. 18

Pesto and Sun-Dried Tomato Torte p. 16

Burgundy Mushrooms p. 23

Scallop Sauté p. 99

Toffee Dip with Apples p. 13

Party Brie Wheel p. 17

Turkish Lamb Kebabs p. 145

Sussex Harvest Supper

Pumpkin Mushroom Soup p. 55

Pork Tenderloin aux Duxelles p. 140

Kahlúa Glazed Carrots p. 163

Broccoli Amandine p. 159

Raw Apple Cake p. 195

Off to the Races
Point-to-Point Picnic

Asparagus-Artichoke-Mushroom Salad p. 76

Brandied Crabmeat Bisque p. 59

Peppercorn Beef Tenderloin p. 129

Wild Rice, Raisins, and Pecans p. 167

One Bowl, No-Knead French Bread p. 42

Bavarian Apple Torte p. 203

In 1960, after visiting Winterthur, first lady Jacqueline Kennedy invited Henry Francis du Pont to head the committee overseeing renovations of the White House.

To Take The Chill Off

Sun-Dried Tomato Mousse p. 14

Rocky Mountain Salad p. 77

Pasta with Lobster and Tarragon p. 100

Chocolate Truffle Loaf with Raspberry Sauce p. 199

For a pretty, casual spring centerpiece, fill a footed bowl with fresh lemons and limes. Pierce several of the lemons with a fork shortly before your guests arrive, to give your room a lovely scent.

Lunch After Longwood

Spinach Quiche p. 49

Black Bean and Rice Salad p. 72

Sesame Noodle Salad p. 85

Marinated Bean Sprout Salad p. 80

Lemon-Almond Buttermilk Bread
with Balsamic Strawberries p. 44

Orange Poppy Seed Cake p. 196

Brandy Slush Punch p. 37

Spring Fling

Three-Way Strawberry-Spinach Salad p. 79

Baby Lamb with Lemon Sauce p. 146

Green Beans with Lemon and Onion p. 161

Holiday Sweet Potatoes p. 169

Apple Cranberry Casserole p. 170

Grasshopper Pie p. 205

Souper Mom Dinner

White Chicken Chili p. 68

Spinach Pear Salad p. 80

Sweet Potato Biscuits p. 45

Amish Whoopie Pies p. 179

♪ *When the kids plan a special meal for Mom.*

❦

Flowers

To extend the life of fresh-cut flowers, be sure that only the stems are submerged; all leaves and flowers should be above the water level in the vase. It is also helpful to do one of the following:

~ Use one part lemon-lime soda (not diet) to three parts water in the vase.

~ Dissolve 1 teaspoon sugar in a gallon of water. Place one aspirin tablet in your vase, then fill with sugar-water mixture and stir to mix thoroughly.

~ Add a drop or two of bleach when filling your vase, to keep bacteria from building up.

~ If nothing has been added, change the water in your vase every other day.

Flowers will also last longer if the vase is kept full; it's a good idea to replenish the water supply daily with ice cubes.

To make chocolate dessert cups, line a muffin tin with paper muffin cups, then paint the inside of each with melted bittersweet chocolate. Chill until firm, then peel off the paper. Fill with sweetened sliced berries, mousse or pudding, and serve on a chilled silver or pewter platter, so the chocolate stays cold and the cups hold their shape.

Notes

Contributors' Names

Christine Bader
Jena Baffone
Sarah Barbour
Glenny Bartram
Margee Begg
Keia Benefield
Charlene Bertheaud
Shelley Boden
Vy Bolhouse
Renee Bosco
Amy Boyd-Kirksey
Beth Brinly
Debbie Brown
Deana Burd
Susan Burton
Adelena Cardone
Peggy Carroll
Cathy Cessna
Jennie Chmiel
Kim Chitty
Susan Cleary
Kate Cowperthwait
Deborah Cuoco
Kate Davis
Lori Diamanty
Kathy Doolin
Diane du Pont
Rebecca Farabaugh
Marianne Feeley
Adrienne Fornoff
Alison Frost
Lathie Gannon
Leslie Gondek
Sally Goodman
Terri Greenley
Lydia Hall
Ruth Hamilton
Susan Hamilton
Karen Hammond
Kay Harrell

Ashley Harris
Katie Harrison
Heather Hayter
Amanda Heberton
Cheryl Heiks
Constance Herlihy
Shiela Himes
Meg Holden
Aline Holler
Tammy Holm
Sally Horne
Bobbe Hoy
Angela Hyman
Elizabeth "Biddy" Jenkins
Ellen Johnson
Laurie Johnson
Suzy Johnson
Alex Keller
Patsy Keller
Nell Kelley
Dana Ketterer
Sherrie Kirtley
Jane Klinger
Anita Knieser
Kristin Landon
Diane Le Dawn Lawson
Leslie Corey Leach
Catherine Mancini
Gina Mancini-Becker
Kimberly Martin
Donna McCreery
Tia McDowell
Harriet McMillan
Lisa McQuarrie
Keva Ann Mendola
Frank Meyer
Hester Meyers
Catherine Miller
Jeannie Miller
Lyn Milliman

Sara Morris
Sisi Morris
Betts Murdison
Laura Nilstoft
Shannon Oates
Diane Paul
Lisa Pearce
Eleanor T. Pease
Jennifer Shroff Pendley
Missy Perkins
Julie Phillips
Sarah M. Poutasse
Lea Purcell
Lisa Quadrini
Jennifer M. Raiford
Barbara C. Reed
Valerie Robino
Dawn Ryan
Gigi Slattery
Jean Smith
Kim Smith
Laura Smith
Susan Stafford
Jamie Stanzione
Gladys Stevens
Cindy Tanner
Deb Thoet
Sheila Thomas
Karla Tobar
Tracy Townsend
Bobbie Ubersax
Deborah F. Walker
Lori Wehmann
Alison Weiss
Jean Western
Maria Wickey
Jane Winston
Mary G. Wolfe
Kate Zabriskie
Lynn Zbranak

Acknowledgements

The Junior League of Wilmington extends its warmest thanks to the following museums in our area, for their assistance in providing information and photographs for *Dancing on the Table*.

Halsey Spruance – Brandywine River Museum

~

Christine Podmaniczky – Brandywine River Museum

~

Jennifer C. Griffin – Deleware Agricultural Museum & Village

~

Suzy Rogers – Hagley Museum and Library

~

Jan Morrill – Historical Society of Delaware

~

Ellen Muenter – Kennett Square Mushroom Festival

~

Pam Carter – Longwood Gardens

~

Francesca Bonny – Nemours

~

Paddy Dietz – Nemours

~

Hillary Holland – Winterthur

~

Cathy Larkin – Winterthur

Sponsors

Thank you to our generous sponsors, who joined in the dance with us...

Heart and Home Gifts

~

Hilton Garden Inn of Kennett Square

~

Chadds Ford Winery

~

Simon Pearce on the Brandywine

~

Everything But the Kitchen Sink

~

The Delaware Office of Economic Development

Bibliography

Anderson, Jean, *1001 Secrets of Great Cooks.* The Berkley Publishing Group, 1995.

Applewhite, Ashton, William R. Evans, III and Andrew Frothingham, *And I Quote.* St. Martin's Press, 1992.

Bartlett, John, *Bartlett's Familiar Quotations.* Little, Brown and Company, 1980.

Bon Appétit magazine

Bremness, Lesley, *Herbs.* Dorling Kindersley Ltd, 1990.

Cooking Light magazine

Crabtree & Evelyn Cook Book, with photographs by Christopher Baker. Stewart, Tabori & Chang, 1989.

"Experience Delaware: 2001-2002 Official State Travel Guide" Distributed by the Delaware Tourism Office.

Heal, Carolyn and Michael Allsop, *Cooking with Spices.* David & Charles, Ltd., 1983.

Hemphill, John and Rosemary, *Herbs: Their Cultivation and Usage.* Sterling Publishing Co., Inc., 1989.

Hodgson, Moira, *Keeping Company.* Prentice Hall Press, 1988.

"The Horseshoe Crab," Ecological Research and Development Group, Inc., Milton, DE.

Labensky, Sarah R., and Alan M. Hause, *On Cooking.* Prentice Hall, 1995.

McLaughlin, Michael, *The Mushroom Book.* Chronicle Books, 1994.

Meyers, Perla, edited by Judy Knipe, *Perla Meyers' Art of Seasonal Cooking.* Simon & Schuster, 1991.

Morris, William and Mary, *The Morris Dictionary of Word and Phrase Origins.* HarperCollins, Publishers, Inc., 1988.

Ridgway, Judy, *The Cheese Companion.* Running Press, 1999.

Rinzler, Carol Ann, *The Complete Book of Herbs, Spices and Condiments.*
   Facts On File, 1990.

State.de.us website

Warner, Carolyn, *The Last Word: A Treasury of Women's Quotes.* Prentice Hall, 1992.

Many thanks to *Phillips Mushroom Farms,* Kennett Square, PA, for providing expert information about mushrooms.

Also with many thanks to the *Delaware Economic Development Office,* and the *Delaware Tourism Office,* for brochures and statistics about the fascinating state of Delaware!

Notes

Index

A

B

Index

Index

Index

O

P

Q

R

Index

S

Dancing on the Table

Thank you for supporting the many community projects
of the Junior League of Wilmington.

Please send me _____ copies   @ $19.95 each _____

Shipping & handling, per copy $ 4.95 each _____

S&H for each additional book to the same address $ 1.50 each _____

                                          TOTAL $ _____

Please print:

Name_____

Address _____

City _____ State _____ Zip _____

_____ Check or money order enclosed, payable to Junior League of Wilmington

_____ Visa _____ MasterCard # _____Exp: _____

Signature: _____

Please mail to:
JLW Cookbook
1801 North Market Street
Wilmington, DE 19802
or
Phone: (302) 652-3700   •   *Fax:* (302) 652-0826
E-Mail: JuniorLeague@diamondnet.org

- -

Dancing on the Table

Thank you for supporting the many community projects
of the Junior League of Wilmington.

Please send me _____ copies   @ $19.95 each _____

Shipping & handling, per copy $ 4.95 each _____

S&H for each additional book to the same address $ 1.50 each _____

                                          TOTAL $ _____

Please print:

Name_____

Address _____

City _____ State _____ Zip _____

_____ Check or money order enclosed, payable to Junior League of Wilmington

_____ Visa _____ MasterCard # _____Exp: _____

Signature: _____

Please mail to:
JLW Cookbook
1801 North Market Street
Wilmington, DE 19802
or
Phone: (302) 652-3700   •   *Fax:* (302) 652-0826
E-Mail: JuniorLeague@diamondnet.org